ENDORSEMENTS

The Joy Book: The Christian's Abundant Joy In The Darkest Nights by Dr. James O. Davis is a masterpiece exposition on the Book of Philippians. I highly recommend this book become your next "must read" and a future "go to" resource when preaching on joy.
—**Rev. Terry Bailey**, District Superintendent, Tennessee Assemblies of God Ministry Network

I believe every Christian desires to know and experience abundant joy, especially when times are hard, or heartbreak has come ones' way. In *The Joy Book: The Christian's Abundant Joy In The Darkest Nights*, Dr. James O. Davis captivates our attention and shows us the path from mere happiness to incredible joy in our daily living. I encourage you to secure a box of books for your family or leadership team.
—**Dr. Doug Beacham**, International Pentecostal Holiness Church, Oklahoma City, Oklahoma

Rejoice in the Lord always and again I say rejoice! These renown words were written by the Apostle Paul in the Book of Philippians from the Mamertine Prison, in the heart of Rome. But how does a Christian experience such resounding joy? Dr. James O. Davis, in *The Joy Book: The Christian's Abundant Joy In The Darkest Nights*, walks us through every chapter and verse in Philippians to show us how to daily experience incredible Christ-centered joy in our lives. You will love book and be able to live the joyful life!
—**Dr. Gustavo Crocker**, Church of the Nazarene, General Superintendent, Lenexa, Kansas

Dr. James O. Davis has written a powerful, in-depth study on the biblical meaning and applications of Christ-centered joy. *The Joy Book: The Christian's Abundant Joy In The Darkest Nights*, is laid out in a memorable, logical format which allows for an easy way for individual and group study. As Christians it is a blessing to see in print how we can have a peace that surpasses all understanding and a hope for our eternal life with The Lord!
—**Dr. Edward Ferrell**, Founder, Village Dental, The Villages, Florida

If any group has a corner on living joyfully it is those who have experienced the saving knowledge of Jesus Christ. The book of Philippians is one of the best sources for cultivating that joy and Dr. James O. Davis has captured the essence of the joy message in this latest work. His years of ministry experience shines through as he unpacks Philippians from a perspective that has perhaps never been done before.
—**Dr. Timothy Hill**, Presiding Bishop, Church of God, Cleveland, TN

The Word of God is like a treasure chest, filled with living treasures, waiting for us to open and discover the very source of a vibrant and abundant Christian life! *The Joy Book: The Christian's Abundant Joy In The Darkest Nights*, written by our truly joyful friend and brother, Dr. James O. Davis, will take you on an adventure into what your heart longs for, ever abiding joy! Dr. Davis writes from an overflow of his personal encounters with the Lord, and as you are reading this book, you too will experience joy encounters with the Holy Spirit. Hope will arise in your heart as you understand that joy is for every believer and is everlasting!

—**Jerry and Sue Horst**, Vanguard Development Group, Lancaster, PA

In Dr. James O. Davis' classic style, he has written a timeless book entitled, *The Joy Book: The Christian's Abundant Joy In The Darkest Nights* is filled with inspirational and practical insights on how we can minister to our communities and the world with joy. I encourage you to read it prayerfully and expectantly!

—**Dr. Suliasi Kurulo**, Founder, World Harvest Center, Suva, Fiji

When an author writes a book on joy I want to know if he really lives that way. In the years that I have known Dr. Davis the strong anchor of his life is his deep joy sourced from the living Word of God. He writes the way he lives. While reading his book you will see that joy is not for just a few, but for you.

—**Dr. Larry Lamb**, Cielo Vista Church
El Paso, Texas

I am delighted to highly recommend James O. Davis' latest publication, *The Joy Book: The Christian's Abundant Joy In The Darkest Nights*. James O. Davis possesses a distinctive ability to eloquently and impactfully elucidate the teachings of the Bible, enriching the reader's understanding and spiritual growth. This book guides the reader toward finding joy amidst challenging circumstances, encouraging a profound sense of tranquillity and positivity.

—**Rev. Joseph Fenech Laudi**, General Superintendent, Assemblies of God of Malta

Through tests and trials, Dr. James Davis personally evidences a profound joy as he works tirelessly to fulfill the Great Commission. In his latest book, Dr. Davis helps us cut through the temporary and self-centered "happiness" our world offers to instead seek that lasting and selfless joy found only in Jesus Christ. He does this by close attention to God's Word, walking you verse by verse through Philippians. With Dr. Davis as your guide, you will find God's truth illuminated here in a memorable, powerful, and applicable way.

—**Dr. Ben Lovvorn**, Executive Pastor, First Baptist Dallas

Dr. James O. Davis' dive into a study of Philippians, and the joy that every Christian can have, is a roadmap to spiritual strength. Satan loves to steal the joy from Believers, and when he does, he steals their strength since, as Scripture says, "the joy of the Lord is our strength." This book is a must read for every Believer seeking to have overwhelming joy and strength in the darkest of times!

—**Dr. Wade Mumm**, Vice President, Assemblies of God Theological Seminary, Senior Pastor, Greene Way Church, Orlando, Florida

In a world with so much pain and sorrow, the ever increase of sin and evil, leaves very little or no room for "Joy". Into this darkness, Dr. James O. Davis lights a bright candle with his latest book, *The Joy Book: The Christian's Abundant Joy In The Darkest Nights*. Like the Apostle Paul who was in a dismal position himself, Dr. Davis urges us to rejoice not in our circumstances but *to rejoice* in the Lord. We are all destined to become more and more like Christ Jesus. Therefore, this volume is a must read for every child of God.

—**Rev. T. L. Roman**, Chairperson,
Assemblies of God Association Southern Cape

In a world pre-occupied with fleeting satisfaction, Dr. James O. Davis masterfully guides readers to discern how joy, rooted in our connection to Jesus Christ, offers a depth of fulfillment far beyond the transient nature of happiness. *The Joy Book: The Christian's Abundant Joy In The Darkest Nights* is a compelling reminder that true contentment springs from holiness, and is a must-read for anyone seeking lasting joy in an ever-changing world. With striking clarity and depth, Dr. Davis journeys through the pages of Philippians to unveil the spiritual significance of the transformative power of joy found in an authentic relationship with Jesus.

—**Mr. A. Larry Ross**, Founder/President, A. Larry Ross Communications, Dallas, TX

Dr. James O. Davis has written on one of the fruits of the Spirit—Joy, which is not only a most misunderstood topic but a missing link in the fabric of our Christian faith. To many believers, Joy is confused with "happenstance"—*The Joy Book* sheds needed light on this. Joy comes from our relationship with Christ and not from external sources. How else can we count it all joy when we fall into diverse temptations? Indeed, you will find great Joy as you read the pages of *The Joy Book*.

—**Rev. John Smith**, Guyana Assemblies of God General Superintendent, George Town, Guyana

Dr. James O. Davis' *The Joy Book* is a must read and wonderfully captures God's higher purpose for the Christian life. Dr. Davis has provided a powerful treatise and fresh insight, along with masterfully unlocking the door to JOY possibilities for the Christian Life. His inspiring work brings the book of Philippians alive for the reader. The spiritual truths of a JOY transcends fleeting happiness and gives victorious outcomes even in the darkest nights of the soul.

—**Chaplain (Major General) Thomas L Solhjem USA**, Retired

Just as Paul and Silas, after being beaten and thrown into a dirty, dark, damp Philippian dungeon, could sing and worship with joy (Acts 16:25), Dr. James O. Davis' book entitled, *The Joy Book: The Christian's Abundant Joy In The Darkest Nights*, on Paul's Roman prison epistle to the Philippians, maps out for us the divine path of how to experience heavenly JOY and live out contagious JOY in the midst of life's challenges and difficulties.

—**Dr. James Hudson Taylor IV**, President, Chinese Theological Seminary, Taipei, Taiwan

The Joy Book: The Christian's Abundant Joy In The Darkest Nights is an outstanding read for every Christian. Every Christian will eventually go through the "midnight hour of the soul" in their life. Dr. James O. Davis has provided the profound principles and personal path to joy, both in the high times and in the hard times. Many Christians have achieved the happiness and healthiness, but this book will help you to also obtain holiness!
—**Dr. Elmer Towns**, Cofounder,
Liberty University, Lynchburg, VA

In a world where Christians face challenges that impact their faith, Dr. James O Davis introduces a revolutionary tool called *The Joy Book* to aid those in ministry. This book not only discusses the concept of joy, but also provides practical insights on how to embody it. It is a valuable resource for all who seek to serve others in their Christian journey, offering a fresh perspective and guidance for navigating obstacles with positivity and grace. And just when readers think they have uncovered all its secrets, *The Joy Book* reveals a surprising twist that challenges their perceptions and deepens their understanding of true joy.
—**Rev. Randall Van Nelson**, Bishop, River Tabernacle, PHCSA

Dr. James Davis is one of the happiest and most positive persons I have ever met. He not only exudes confidence in the One He believes, but also a deep sense of joyful contentment. I have never in all my interactions with him ever see him sulky, moody or frustrated. He is one joyful trooper. Within the pages of this book, we will embark on a journey to explore the many facets of JOY, its source, its manifestation and its power. May the Holy Spirit develop this amazing fruit in your life as you journey through the pages of this transformational book!
—**Rev. Yang Tuck Yoong**, Senior Pastor,
Cornerstone Community Church, Singapore, Chairman,
The Alliance of Pentecostal and Charismatic
Churches in Singapore

The Book of Philippians was authored by St. Paul whilst caged in a Roman prison located in the center of the Roman Empire, to the brothers and sisters of the Philippians Church located in what used to be an important center of the late Greek Empire, to be joyous of the final destination: "The Kingdom of God." Dr. James O. Davis' *The Joy Book: The Christian's Abundant Joy In The Darkest Nights* is a must-read for all Christians who want to be joyous in the Kingdom of God. Read it and find true joy!

—**Dr. Byoungho Zoh**, Founder, Tongdok Bible, Seoul, Korea

THE JOY BOOK

The Christian's Abundant Joy
In The Darkest Nights

JAMES O. DAVIS

Foreword by Carla Sunberg

Unless otherwise indicated, all Scripture quotations are taken from the *New American Standard Bible,* Copyright © The Lockman Foundation 1960, 1962, 1963, 1968, 1971, 1972, 1973, 1975, 1977, 1995. Used by permission.

Scripture quotations marked (KJV) are taken from the King James Version of the Bible. Public domain.

Scripture quotations marked (TLB) are taken from The Living Bible copyright © 1971 by Tyndale House Foundation. Used by permission of Tyndale House Publishers Inc., Carol Stream, Illinois 60188. All rights reserved.

The Joy Book

Copyright © 2024 by Dr. James O. Davis

ISBN: 979-8-9855197-2-3

Billion Soul Publishing
Orlando, Florida
www.billionsoulpub.com

Contents and/or cover may not be reproduced in whole or part in any form without written consent of the author.

DEDICATION

To Mrs. Marjorie Paul Who

Lived For Her Lord, Loved Her Husband,
Led Her Daughter And Granddaughters,
And Left A Legacy For A Lifetime!

I Am A Better Man And Have A Brighter Mind
Because She Cared For Me Like Her Own Son,
And Communicated With Me Regarding Eternity!

TABLE OF CONTENTS

Foreword by Dr. Karla Sunberg..xxiii
Introduction...xxv
    A. What Is Joy? xxv
    B. What Is Happiness?...xxvi
    C. Differences Between Joy and Happiness xxvii
        1. Constant: Joy is constant while happiness is temporary..xxvii
        2. Compassion: Joy is about selflessness while happiness involves pleasing self....................xxvii
        3. Commitment: Joy is deeply spiritual while happiness lacks depth......................................xxviii
        4. Circumspect: Joy is meaningful while happiness feels good...xxviii
        5. Choice: Joy is a choice a person makes while others chase after happiness...........................xxix
        6. Challenges: Joy involves trials and hardships while happiness is easier to achieve................xxix
        7. Constructive: Joy is transformative while happiness can hold us back xxx
        8. Connect: Joy connects people to each other while happiness consists of momentary connections..xxx

    9. Costly: Joy is a less common satisfying feeling than happiness is xxxi
    10. Communicate: Joy is difficult to define while happiness is easy to describe xxxi
    11. Consistent: Joy can exist in the midst of difficulties while happiness cannot live in this reality xxxi
  D. How to Find Our True Joy xxxii

The Positives of the Christian Life (Philippians 1:1-11)

Chapter 1: The Eternal Family of God (Philippians 1:1-6; 2:1; 3:10) 3
  A. The Supernatural Formation of the Family of God (Philippians 1:1) 4
    1. The Restraint of the Spirit 4
    2. The Release of the Spirit 5
    3. The Results of the Spirit 6
  B. The Sacred Fellowship in the Family of God (Philippians 1:1-5) 7
    1. The Fellowship of Soul-Winning 8
    2. The Fellowship of Supplication (Philippians 2:1) 8
    3. The Fellowship of Suffering (Philippians 3:10) 8
  C. The Secure Future for the Family of God (Philippians 1:6) 9

Chapter 2: Servants and Saints (Philippians 1:1-2,10,13) 11
  A. We Need to Lead as Servants (Philippians 1:1) 12
  B. We Need to Live as Saints (Philippians 1:1-2,10) 14

Chapter 3: Joyful Heart Surgery (Philippians 1:3-8,13; 2:1; 4:6) 19
  A. We Can Have the Comfort of Communion (Philippians 1:5,7; 2:1) 21
  B. We Can Have the Confidence of Completion (Philippians 1:5-6) 23

    C. We Can Have the Consciousness of Compassion (Philippians 1:8) 26

Chapter 4: The Hallelujah Prayer! (Philippians 1:4,9-11) 29
    A. We Need to Incorporate the Foundation of Prayer 30
        1. Prayer is a personal 30
        2. Prayer is powerful 31
        3. Prayer is purposeful 31
    B. We Need to Include the Formula of Prayer (Philippians 1:9-10) 32
        1. Growing Christians (Philippians 1:9) 32
        2. Genuine Christians (Philippians 1:10) 33
        3. Good Christians (Philippians 1:11) 35
    C. We Need to Be Inspired With the Faith of Prayer (Philippians 1:11) 36
        1. Goal of prayer 36
        2. Dynamics of prayer 36

The Preaching of the Christian Life (Philippians 1:12-20)

Chapter 5: Turning Chains into Gains (Philippians 1:5,12-27) 41
    A. We Have Opportunities to Extend the Gospel (Philippians 1:12-13; 4:22) 43
    B. We Have Opportunities to Encourage Others (Philippians 1:14-18) 45
    C. We Have Opportunities to Exalt Christ (Philippians 1:19-20) 48

Chapter 6: The Paradigms of a Prisoner (Philippians 1:12,21-26) 51
    A. We Need to Develop a Powerful Philosophy 52
        1. Personally Alive (Philippians 1:21) 52
        2. Practically Alive 53
        3. Presently Alive 54
        4. Potentially Alive 54
    B. We Need a Productive Personhood 56

      1. Indispensable (Philippians 1:12,22,24-26) 57
      2. Inspirational (Philippians 1:22,25) 58
      3. Invaluable (Philippians 1:22) 59
  C. We Need a Positiveness for Problems (Philippians 1:21-23) 59
      1. A Delightful Dilemma (Philippians 1:23) 60
      2. A Divine Departure (Philippians 1:21) 62

Chapter 7: Living Like We Are Dying (Philippians 1:5,12,20-21,27-30) 65
  A. Our Conduct Must Be Consistent (Philippians 1:27) 66
  B. Our Courage Must Be Evident (Philippians 1:27-28) 68
  C. Our Christlikeness Must Be Triumphant (Philippians 1:29-30) 71

The Patterns of the Christian Life (Philippians 2:1-30)

Chapter 8: Others (Philippians 2:1-4,21) 77
  A. We Should Encourage Harmony in the Church (Philippians 2:2) 81
  B. We Should Embrace Humility in the Church (Philippians 2:3) 82
  C. We Should Exemplify Helpfulness in the Church (Philippians 2:2,4,21) 85

Chapter 9: The God-Man (Philippians 2:5-11) 89
  A. Jesus Is the Supernatural Son of God (Philippians 2:6-7) 91
  B. Jesus Is the Sinless Son of God (Philippians 2:8) 92
  C. Jesus Is the Sovereign Son of God (Philippians 2:6) 93
  D. Jesus Is the Sacrificial Son of God (Philippians 2:8) 95
  E. Jesus Is the Striving Son of God (Philippians 2:9) 97
  F. Jesus Is the Soon-Coming Son of God (Philippians 2:9-11) 97
  G. Jesus Is the Saving Son of God (Philippians 2:8) 99

Chapter 10: The Inside Job (Philippians 2:8,12-13) **101**
   A. We Have a Grand Possession (Philippians 2:12)........ 102
      1. God planned our salvation 103
      2. God promised our salvation 103
      3. God procured our salvation 103
      4. God presents our salvation...................................... 103
   B. We Have a Godly Process (Philippians 2:12)............... 104
      1. The activity of the process 104
      2. The attitude of the process (Philippians 2:12) 106
   C. We Have a Glorious Power (Philippians 2:13) 106
      1. God uses the Word of God...................................... 107
      2. God uses prayer in our life 108
      3. God uses our sorrows, suffering,
         and heartaches 108

Chapter 11: Shining Like Stars in the Universe (Philippians 2:14-17) **111**
   A. Our Light Enlightens Others
     (Philippians 2:14-15) 112
   B. Our Light Expands Everywhere 115
      1. We are to overcome darkness
        (Philippians 2:15) 115
      2. We are to offer direction (Philippians 2:16) 117
   C. Our Light Expels Energy (Philippians 2:17)................ 117

Chapter 12: Passing Joy To Others (Philippians 2:4, 19-22) **121**
   A. We Are Sons (Philippians 2:22) 123
      1. We are shaped.. 123
      2. We are saved... 125
      3. We are seasoned 126
   B. We Are to Be Servants (Philippians 2:22).................... 126
      1. We have a calling (Philippians 2:19-21) 127
      C. We are to be concerned (Philippians 1:21;
         2:20-21) 128
      3. We are to cooperate (Philippians 2:22) 129
   C. We Are to Be a Substitute (Philippians 2:19,22)......... 129

Chapter 13: Knocking on Death's Door for Christ (Philippians 1:5,12,27; 2:25-28; 4:18) **133**
   A. We Are to be Stable Christians (Philippians 2:25; 1:5,12,27) 134
   B. We Are to Be Sacrificial Christians (Philippians 2:26-27; 4:18) 135
      1. Dissipation 137
      2. Discipline (Philippians 2:26-27) 137
   C. We Are to Be Significant Christians (Philippians 2:28) 139

The Prize of the Christian Life (Philippians 3:1-21)

Chapter 14: The Great Exchange (Philippians 3:1-9) **143**
   A. The Old Math of Life (Philippians 3:4) 146
      1. Our Rituals (Philippians 3:5) 146
      2. Our Relationships (Philippians 3:5) 146
      3. Our Respectability (Philippians 3:5) 146
      4. Our Race (Philippians 3:5) 147
      5. Our Religion (Philippians 3:5) 147
      6. Our Reputation (Philippians 3:6-7) 147
   B. The New Math With the Lord (Philippians 3:7-9) 148
      1. Our Burden for Christ 150
         a. Financial cost 150
         b. Fitness cost 150
         c. Family cost 151
      2. Our Benefits with Christ 152
         a. The Knowledge of Christ (Philippians 3:8) 152
         b. The Fellowship of Christ (Philippians 3:9) 152
         c. The Righteousness Through Christ 152

Chapter 15: That I May Know Christ (Philippians 3:10-11) **155**
   A. Our Relationship to Christ Brings Power Into Our Life (Philippians 3:10) 156
      1. A Desirable Power (Philippians 3:10) 156

      2. A Demonstrated Power 157
  B. Our Relationship With Christ Brings Pain Into Our Life
    (Philippians 3:10) 159
      1. Social Pain 159
      2. Emotional Pain 160
      3. Physical Pain 160
      4. Spiritual Pain (Philippians 3:10) 160
  C. Our Relationship With Christ Brings Purpose Into
    Our Life 161
      1. Our Immediate Purpose (Philippians 3:10) 161
      2. Our Ultimate Purpose (Philippians 3:11) 162

Chapter 16: Winning the Christian Race (Philippians 3:12-15) 165
  A. Finding Christ in the Race (Philippians 3:12) 166
      1. Apprehend 166
      2. Apprehensive 167
  B. Following Christ in the Race 168
      1. Concentration on the Present
         (Philippians 3:13) 168
      2. Obliteration of the Past (Philippians 3:13) 170
      3. Pressing Toward the Mark 171
  C. Finishing for Christ in the Race (Philippians 3:14) 172
      1. The Mark to Reach (Philippians 3:14) 172
      2. The Medal to Reward 172

Chapter 17: The Heavenly-Minded Leader (Philippians 3:8,14,17-21) 175
  A. Managing Earthly Things (Philippians 3:17-18) 176
      1. Every Life Has a Destiny (Philippians 3:19) 177
      2. Every Life Has a Deity (Philippians 3:19) 178
      3. Every Life Has a Depravity
         (Philippians 3:18-19) 179
  B. Minding Heavenly Things (Philippians 3:20) 180
      1. Our Heavenly Citizenship 180
      2. Our Heavenly Anticipation
         (Philippians 3:20) 182

    3. Our Heavenly Transformation
(Philippians 3:21) 182

The Peace of the Christian Life (Philippians 4:1-9)

Chapter 18: How to Heal a Church Fight (Philippians 1:3-4; 2:5; 4:1-3) 187
    A. An Appeal to the Enriched People 188
        1. Cultivate a Christian Atmosphere Through Community 189
        2. Cultivate a Christian Atmosphere Through Compassion (Philippians 4:1) 189
        3. Cultivate a Christian Atmosphere Through Celebration 190
        4. Commit to a Christian Advance (Philippians 4:1) 190
    B. An Address to an Estrangement Problem (Philippians 2:5; 4:2-3) 191
    C. An Appeal to an Excellent Peacemaker (Philippians 4:3) 194
    D. An Ask for an Eternal Perspective (Philippians 4:3) 195
        1. The scope 196
        2. The salvation 196
        3. The sentence 196

Chapter 19: The Mental Makeover (Philippians 4:4-9,11) 197
    A. Rejoice in the Presence of the Lord (Philippians 4:4-5) 198
    B. Rely on the Power of God (Philippians 4:6) 200
        1. Worry is worthless 200
        2. Worry is wasteful 201
        3. Worry is wicked 202
    C. Reflect on the Provision of the Lord (Philippians 4:6) 202

    D. Rest in the Peace of the Lord (Philippians 4:7) 203
    E. Renew in the Purpose of God (Philippians 4:8) 204
        1. The Reliance Test (Philippians 4:8) 205
        2. The Respect Test (Philippians 4:8) 205
        3. The Rightness Test (Philippians 4:8) 205
        4. The Reverence Test (Philippians 4:8) 205
        5. The Relationship Test (Philippians 4:8) 206
        6. The Refinement Test (Philippians 4:8-9) 206

The Provisions of the Christian Life (Philippians 4:10-23)

Chapter 20: The Community of Contentment (Philippians 1:12-13; 4:10-13,22) 211
    A. We Should Rejoice in Our Provisions (Philippians 4:10,12) 212
    B. We Should Rest in Our Possessions (Philippians 4:11) 214
        1. Self-Satisfaction 215
        2. Self-Sufficiency 215
        3. Savior-Sufficiency 216
        4. Accept Our Situation 217
        5. Adapt to Our Surroundings (Philippians 4:12) 217
        6. Appropriate Our Success (Philippians 1:12-13, 4:22) 218
    C. We Should Realize Our Power (Philippians 4:13) 219
        1. We Move From Pessimism (Philippians 4:13) 219
        2. We Move From Presumption 219
        3. We Move to Power 219

Chapter 21: According to God's Riches in Glory (Philippians 1:1,3; 4:1,15,17-19,22-23) 223
    A. We Need to Invest in the Beauty of Giving 224
        1. Blesses Others (Philippians 4:15) 224
        2. Enriches Us (Philippians 4:17) 225
        3. Pleases God (Philippians 4:18) 226

- a. Our Walk in Life 227
- b. Our Worship to the Lord 227
- c. Our Winning of the Lost 227
- B. We Need to Be Inspired by the Bounty of God (Philippians 4:19) 228
  1. The Source of Our Supply (Philippians 4:19) 228
     - a. Rich in Goodness 228
     - b. Rich in Grace 228
     - c. Rich in Glory 229
  2. The Scope of Our Supply 229
     - a. Our Material Needs 229
     - b. Our Emotional Needs 230
     - c. Our Spiritual Needs 230
     - d. Our Physical Needs 230
  3. The Standard of Our Supply (Philippians 4:19) ... 231
- C. We Need Interest in the Benediction of Grace (Philippians 4:23) 232
  1. Emancipating Grace 232
  2. Ennobling Grace (Philippians 4:22) 232
  3. Enabling Grace (Philippians 4:23; 1:1) 232

Conclusion—The Stolen Song of Joy 235
- A. We Need to Refrain From the Sad Misery of a Captured Christian 236
- B. We Need to Reflect on the Stinging Memory of a Captured Christian 238
- C. We Need to Remember the Sarcastic Mockery of a Captured Christian 239
- D. We Need to Refuse the Silenced Melody of a Captured Christian 240

FOREWORD

As a child attending Sunday School, I learned to sing the song, "I've got the joy, joy, joy, joy down in my heart." With enthusiasm, we would shout out, "Where?" and respond, "down in my heart" and finally, "down in my heart to stay." There was something about this concept of joy that was beginning to form in our minds that should have remained with us throughout the entirety of our lives. Sadly, that's not always the case, because for many, this idea of a deep-down joy in our hearts has been replaced by the world's idea of happiness. They are not one and the same, and that's the reality we encounter when we take the time to study what God's word tells us about joy. This is the journey that Dr. James O. Davis places before us: one that examines the difference between God's desire for us to experience joy, and the empty promises of happiness coming from the world.

From Genesis through Revelation, we read about God's desire for humankind to experience radical transformation and to develop an intimacy with Christ. God's longing is for each human, male and female, who were created in the image of God, to be living reflections of that image. As living reflections, the characteristics of God become visible through how we interact and react to our experiences in life. Those interactions are to produce the fruit of the Spirit, one of which is joy. This becomes evident as we travel through life with the Lord, and experience ever-increasing nearness to Him.

The invitation from this book leads to a deeper walk, one in which we will experience the "down in my heart" kind of joy. *The Joy Book: The Christian's Abundant Joy In The Darkest Nights*, hones in on Paul's theme of joy found in his letter to the church in Philippi. As ministers, we're not supposed to have a favorite church, but most of us have had one—or at least a favorite ministry assignment, where somehow things just came together and "clicked." Many scholars have speculated that this is how Paul may have felt about the church in Philippi. Just possibly, he experienced the deep-down joy while ministering alongside Lydia, the jailer and his family, and so many others. Whatever his reasons, Paul leaves us with much to be mined, throughout his entire Epistle of Philippians, that will help us on our journey of Joy.

Dr. Davis has already done the hard work for us, through this beautiful volume, that invites us to find the joy that will stay with us regardless of the circumstances or conditions, the problems or the pains, and the failing or the faltering. As you read this life-changing book, you will be lifted to the level of "Rejoice in the Lord always and again I say rejoice."

Dr. Davis and I have served together in many different leadership capacities. In a world trite on truth and shallow in service, he has brought joyful leadership into my life, in particular, and the Body of Christ, in general. You will love *The Joy Book: The Christian's Abundant Joy In The Darkest Nights*. You are going to know how to have the joy, joy, joy down in my heart!

—**Dr. Carla Sunberg**
General Superintendent
Church of the Nazarene
April, 2024

INTRODUCTION

Happiness depends on what transpires, but joy enriches the soul and comes only from the Lord. Truly, *the joy of the* Lord *is your strength* (Nehemiah 8:10).

As we begin our joy journey together, it important that we come to cognitive clarity as to what the differences are between happiness and joy. Much labor has gone into this book—not to help us to be happier but hopefully to help us to be full of joy. Learning the differences between happiness and joy can help us live a more meaningful life filled with greater purpose.

The Lord does want us to be happy and healthy, but holiness is the Lord's higher aim for our lives. In like manner, while the Lord desires that we be happy and satisfied, joy and fulfillment are at a much deeper level. Joy can be highly gratifying in a way that is not selfish, whereas happiness is wrapped up in what makes us happy.

WHAT IS JOY?

Joy is a **selfless feeling of extreme happiness and pleasure.** We may have joy when we care for others, are thankful or grateful, and have deep spiritual experiences. While joy often requires great self-sacrifice, we will find lasting inward contentment and peace. Furthermore, this feeling may not be about ourselves but about helping others become more content.

True joy cannot be achieved without Christ in our lives. In the Book of Philippians, the Apostle Paul uses the words "rejoice" or "joyful" 16 times in 104 verses. He was not giving pep talks on joy to indicate that a person could work joy up in their lives. In every instance, rejoicing or joyfulness was connected to Christ.

Holiness is the Lord's higher aim for our lives.

Whenever we are at our lowest point, we should turn to Christ in order to be filled with joy. When we feel alone and as if no one is on our side, we can turn to prayer to help us through any problems we face. When we find our spiritual equilibrium, we also find joy deep in our soul that is almost unbelievable and indescribable.

WHAT IS HAPPINESS?

Happiness is an emotion that allows us to experience various feelings such as pleasure, contentment, bliss, and satisfaction. We may feel happy when we gain material possessions or have earthly experiences. Although happiness is temporary, it is about our own pleasure and causes us to express outward elation.

For example, we feel happiness when we are hungry and then eat our favorite foods. Despite the fact that this particular experience is nowhere near joy, it **puts us in a positive state of mind**. At other times, we can experience happiness when we float an idea and our peers accept it. However, happiness comes and goes.

INTRODUCTION

DIFFERENCES BETWEEN JOY AND HAPPINESS

When we imagine what joy and happiness are, we might not perceive any clear distinctions at first. However, after thinking more deeply about it, we will likely come to the conclusion that the two words are exceptionally unique from each other.

Constant: Joy is constant while happiness is temporary.

For example, having a baby can make a person joyous—a feeling can last forever. While winning a new car will definitely make us happy, the feeling is temporary because it will eventually become only a memory. *The Joy Book* will assist in understanding how the Apostle Paul gained the joy that renewed him—even in prison. When we have joy, we will not find ourselves chasing rainbows of happiness.

Compassion: Joy is about selflessness while happiness involves pleasing self.

Being selfless can mean ignoring our own feelings in order to benefit someone else. Although this can be a challenge, we can gain joy, meaning, and purpose from it. For example, joyous feelings may arise when we care for someone we love when they need us the most.

Paul illustrated selflessness through Epaphroditus who risked his life for the sake of the gospel and for the Philippians. He told them to honor such a man. Paul also taught us that his joy was complete through his relationship with the Philippians.

Happiness can be fun but definitely not as meaningful because it is only about pleasing ourselves. If we go out to eat at a particular restaurant, it could make us happy but would not necessarily be a particularly fulfilling activity. However, if we cook a meal to take to someone who is less fortunate or is experiencing illness, we will find a joyful fulfillment.

Commitment: Joy is deeply spiritual while happiness lacks depth.

*Then he said to them, "Go, eat of the fat, drink of the sweet, and send portions to him who has nothing prepared; for this day is holy to our Lord. Do not be grieved, for the joy of the L*ORD *is your strength"* (Nehemiah 8:10).

The joy of the Lord is found on the road to restoration.

The joy of the Lord is found on the road to restoration. God convicts us of sin, and our first reaction is often guilt and shame. Ezra the scribe gathered all the people and read to them from the book of the law, and the Levites explained the law. *They read from the book, from the law of God, translating to give the sense so that they understood the reading* (Nehemiah 8:8).

The original Hebrew word for "joy" in Nehemiah 8:10 means gladness. The root word of strength means "to be strong, prevail; to make firm, strengthen." The joy of the Lord is a constant gladness and cause to rejoice. It stems from an inner strengthening from our relationship with Him.

Circumspect: Joy is meaningful while happiness feels good.

Since joyful experiences are deep, they can also be meaningful and memorable. For instance, we would likely always remember holding our child's hand for the first time or hearing our spouse laugh. While buying new clothes can feel good at the moment, they are only material objects. However, joy is wrapped up in Jesus Christ, family, people, and close colleagues. God never does His deepest work in the shallowest parts of our lives.

INTRODUCTION

Choice: Joy is a choice a person makes while others chase after happiness.

When we are immature, we often think we want certain things to make us happy; but we do not understand the consequences. When people get what they want, they often find they do not actually want it.

God never does His deepest work in the shallowest parts of our lives.

For example, a man might chase after a woman because she is attractive and makes him smile and laugh. However, this can be a problem because the man is immature and only sees the woman's appearance and personality. The relationship may not endure because it started out for the wrong reasons.

Additionally, no one should have to chase after someone to make them love them. With maturity, a man or woman can consciously choose a partner with whom they share a genuinely mutual connection that can become a truly joyful experience.

Challenges: Joy involves trials and hardships while happiness is easier to achieve.

Taking care of a baby involves plenty of joy but also hard work, dedication, and selflessness. Alternatively, we can make things easier on ourselves by working less and settling for happiness. This means we can be happy by eating an ice cream cone. It is inexpensive and tasty, but we probably will not get much else out of it.

Joy is a selfless feeling of extreme happiness and pleasure. When we work hard, we have better experiences (volunteering, a purposeful career, etc.) that bring joy while happy experiences such as carnival rides and dressing in trendy clothes can become completely meaningless. In other words, happiness can come and go; but true joy can go with us throughout the entirety of our lives.

Constructive: Joy is transformative while happiness can hold us back.

Joyful experiences like marrying, having a family, and sharing a deep Christian life (such as praying together every day, attending church services regularly, etc.) give new depth to life.

Alternatively, happy experiences are not as intense or worthwhile and will likely not provoke any profound feelings that are life-changing. For example, riding in a limousine could make us happy, but the feeling will wear off with nothing left to show but wasted time; and wasting time on meaningless activities holds us back from making personal progress.

Obviously, there is nothing wrong with having fun with friends; but to add value to people's lives, there must be a sense of joy and personal fulfillment.

Connect: Joy connects people to each other while happiness consists of momentary connections.

Getting married and having a family whom we love and focus on in a positive way can bring joy into our life and help us make meaningful connections that will last a lifetime, such as a best friend who loves us for who we are and does not try to change us.

An example of a happy connection can be making friends in college with people who share our interests at the moment. We go to college football games; and while we are together, there is great laughter, excitement, and cheering. These experiences and others like them build great memories and can cause reflection over those moments for years to come.

However, joy that comes from Christ and our relationship with Him as well as with other committed Christians will have a much deeper impact on our souls.

INTRODUCTION

Costly: Joy is a less common satisfying feeling than happiness is.

One reason joy occurs less often is because it takes a great deal of maturity, selflessness, and effort. Since happiness is easier to achieve, it follows that we can be happy more frequently than joyful.

The greatest joy comes from our relationship with Christ.

Even though there is no doubt there is a level of true joy in the world, the greatest joy comes from our relationship with Christ and when we are in sync with Him. Christian joy is far less common and contains stronger feelings than happiness.

Communicate: Joy is difficult to define while happiness is easy to describe.

The intensity associated with joyous experiences can make it difficult to describe. In fact, we would likely have to actually experience joy in order to truly understand how it feels. Apart from this, happy experiences are not nearly as deep; and most of us, if not all, have experienced them at one time or another. This can make them quite simple to describe.

Though you have not seen Him, you love Him, and though you do not see Him now, but believe in Him, you greatly rejoice with joy inexpressible and full of glory (1 Peter 1:8). According to Peter, this joy is not based on what we have seen but comes from Christ in such a manner that is inexpressible and glorious. This is rare indeed!

Consistent: Joy can exist in the midst of difficulties while happiness cannot live in this reality.

We can feel so intensely alone and empty that it makes it impossible to be happy, but having solid Christian beliefs at this time can make us profoundly joyful. Even though happiness is gone, joy can still be present in Christ.

Weeping may last for the night, but a shout of joy comes in the morning (Psalm 30:5). Just as the sun rises out of the darkness, joy rises in our hearts! Money, fame, or health cannot bring us this kind of joy.

HOW TO FIND OUR TRUE JOY

Since finding our true joy can give us a better life, we should walk this path each day. *The Joy Book: The Christian's Abundant Joy in the Darkest Days* will teach us how to discover this joy, develop this joy, and deploy this joy in our lives.

Comparing joy versus happiness can change your life for the better.

As you read through this book, highlight every meaningful sentence and consider keeping a journal. Writing down your thoughts can be helpful in piecing them together and clarifying them. Committing to writing every day can give you an opportunity to see how your thoughts and feelings change over time.

Once you have figured out the personal applications to discovering joy, you can work towards incorporating those things into your life. You can figure out ways to put away the things that do not contribute to your future. These could be bad habits or even negative people who prevent you from obtaining pure joy. Strive to be authentic with yourself and others. With this mind, you will be able to focus on understanding yourself and your wants and needs on a deeper level.

As you read through this book, discuss the truths you have learned with friends. The more you discuss things with others, the clearer they become and the better the applications.

INTRODUCTION

Comparing joy versus happiness can change your life for the better and give you the chance to be better informed in order to create the future you truly want. If joy is what you want, make this a goal and write down the steps to achieve it.

THE POSITIVES OF THE CHRISTIAN LIFE (PHILIPPIANS 1:1-11)

1

THE ETERNAL FAMILY OF GOD

What does a Jewish philosopher who hates Christ, a New Ager who has been deep into the occult, a prison guard whose heart is filled with malignity and hate against all humankind, and a feminist who owns her own business and has never married have in common? All these people were members of the church at Philippi. The Jewish philosopher was the Apostle Paul who had a miraculous conversion experience. The New Ager was a demon-possessed girl who was saved and delivered through the power of Christ. The prison guard was a jailer who was saved in a Philippian revival. The businesswoman was Lydia from Thyatira who traded in purple dyes and fabric for which the city of Thyatira was noted.

The incredible thing is that the grace of God took people from divergent backgrounds and made them one in the Lord Jesus Christ. That is what a church is today—a family of people who come from different backgrounds with different beliefs, ideas, and ideals but who find unity in the family of God. The common denominator in the church is Jesus. Because we have one Lord, we have one life; and because we have one Lord and one life, we have one love—the Lord Jesus Christ. We are the family of God.

The grace of God took people from divergent backgrounds and made them one in the Lord Jesus Christ.

There are so many people who have no family. The Apostle Paul really did not have a family. He had a wife at one time, but we do not know what happened to her. We do not know whether Lydia, the seller of purple, was divorced, widowed, or never married. The demon-possessed girl who was delivered by the power of God needed a family as did the brutal jailer. There are multitudes of people in this world who need a family, and that is what the church is—an extended and eternal family.

THE SUPERNATURAL FORMATION OF THE FAMILY OF GOD

Philippians 1:1 shows how the formation of God's forever family began. *Paul and Timothy, bond-servants of Christ Jesus, To all the saints in Christ Jesus who are in Philippi.*

How did *all the saints* get to be saints? There are only two categories of people in the world: the saints (those who are saved) and the ain'ts (those who are not saved). Luke records the supernatural formation of the church in Acts 16.

The Restraint of the Spirit

The people of the world can build buildings and form organizations; however, there is a dimension to the church that cannot be explained by a program, a personality, propaganda, or planning. If it is not supernatural, it will be superficial.

> *They* [Paul and Silas] *passed through the Phrygian and Galatian region, having been forbidden by the Holy Spirit to speak the word in Asia; and after they came to Mysia, they were trying to go into Bithynia, and the Spirit of Jesus did not permit them* (Acts 16:6-7).

If we are not interested in the restraint of the Spirit, we will never know the release of the Spirit.

Paul and Silas desired to serve the Lord. Their motive was right—to preach the gospel of Jesus. They were going into Asia with a plan to go to Bithynia; but the Holy Spirit said, "No, I don't want you to go that way."

Have you ever taught a teenager how to drive? What is the first thing you show them—the accelerator or the brake? The brake, of course. If they had said, "I'm not interested in the brake," you would probably have said, "Then give me the keys back!"

Before God will ever show us the accelerator, He will always show us the brake. If we are not interested in the restraint of the Spirit, we will never know the release of the Spirit. The path of life is strewn with the wrecks of those who have high-powered engines but faulty brakes. They do not know how to listen to God's "NO." God's no is as important as God's go. Someone once said, "A fanatic is someone who, having lost sight of his goal, increases his speed."

The Release of the Spirit

First God said, "No," and then God said, "Go."

A vision appeared to Paul in the night: a man of Macedonia was standing and appealing to him, and saying, "Come over to Macedonia and help us." When he had seen the vision, immediately we sought to go into Macedonia, concluding that God had called us to preach the gospel to them (Acts 16:9-10).

God does not always give us what we want, but He does give us something better. Paul assayed to go to Bithynia and into Asia; but the Holy Spirit said, "I want you to go over to Greece—to Macedonia" (Acts 16:7-10). God opened up all of Europe for the preaching of the gospel because God was supernaturally building His Church.

The Results of the Spirit

When Paul and Silas got to Philippi, they met Lydia from Thyatira. She came to a prayer meeting, and God touched her heart. She said, "Paul, come over to my house. We'll have a prayer meeting, and you can start your Bible study here." That was the beginning of the church. Soul-winning takes on a new dimension when we know the restraint and the release of the Spirit.

A demon-possessed girl followed Paul around the city of Philippi crying, *These men are bond-servants of the Most High God* (Acts 16:17). Paul had tried to avoid her because we are called to resist the devil, not to chase him; however, Paul had had enough. He turned around and rebuked her in the name of Jesus. The devil came out of her, and she was saved.

Afterwards, Paul and Silas wound up in jail because she was making a lot of money for the men who owned her. They were in the innermost jail at midnight—praising God and giving Him glory. The other prisoners had heard a lot of moaning and groaning but had never heard praising. They had heard a lot of cursing but had probably never heard praying. God was so pleased that He looked down and began to shake the whole jail with an earthquake. As the jail began to shake, the bonds fell off; and the jailer, no doubt a hardened prison guard, was ready to commit suicide. However, Paul and Silas said, "Don't hurt yourself! We're all here! Don't commit suicide! We want to tell you about Jesus"; and the jailer got saved. When a church gets right with God, the devil cannot stop the revival no matter how much persecution comes. All he does is just move locations. There was a revival in that jail that night.

We have a common Lord, a common life, and a common love.

Paul was a philosopher. What is the answer to the intellectual sophistication of our age? Jesus. Lydia was a businesswoman. What is the answer to the deepest needs of a woman's heart? Jesus. The demon-possessed girl was in the grip of the occult. What is the answer to the occult? Jesus. The jailer was surrounded by prisoners and criminals. What is the answer to the crime problem? Jesus.

That is the way God puts people together in a "forever family."

THE SACRED FELLOWSHIP IN THE FAMILY OF GOD

Paul and Timothy, bond-servants of Christ Jesus, To all the saints in Christ Jesus who are in Philippi, including the overseers and deacons: Grace to you and peace from God our Father and the Lord Jesus Christ. I thank my God in all my remembrance of you always offering prayer with joy in my every prayer for you all in view of your participation in the gospel from the first day until now (Philippians 1:1-5).

Your participation in the gospel (v.5). A supernatural formation always leads to sweet fellowship. What is our fellowship? Not coffee and cookies but the gospel of our Lord and Savior Jesus Christ. What is the bond that holds us together? The word *fellowship* or *koinonia* in the Greek means "to have something in common." We have a common Lord, a common life, and a common love.

Koinonia is used three times in Philippians.

The Fellowship of Soul-Winning

In verse 5, Paul speaks of the *koinonia* of the gospel, the *participation* in the gospel—the good news of Jesus Christ. If we want fellowship with someone, we need to look around and find a brother or a sister who is interested in spreading the gospel of Jesus Christ. We need to find someone who wants to win somebody to Jesus. Two people who win a third person to Jesus Christ are never the same again.

The Fellowship of Supplication

Therefore if there is any encouragement in Christ, if there is any consolation of love, if there is any fellowship of the Spirit (Philippians 2:1). If we want fellowship, we need to find a prayer partner and study the Word of God with that person and let the Spirit of God meld us together. Too many churches are wired together, rusted together, or frozen together when they need to be melded together by the Holy Spirit. Two people who pray together are never the same afterwards. When we bind our hearts together in prayer, we will find the *koinonia* of the Spirit.

The Fellowship of Suffering

That I may know Him and the power of His resurrection and the fellowship of His sufferings, being conformed to His death (Philippians 3:10). If we say, "I don't have any friends; I'm not a part of the church," then we need to find someone who is hurting and hurt with them.

Paul said, "I want to know the fellowship of Christ's sufferings." How can we know that? Jesus said, *Truly I say to you, to the extent that you did it to one of these brothers of Mine, even the least of them, you did it to Me* (Matthew 25:40). Two people who win a soul together are never quite the same again; two people who pray together are never quite the same again; and two people who cry together are never quite the same again.

THE SECURE FUTURE FOR THE FAMILY OF GOD

For I am confident of this very thing, that He who began a good work in you will perfect it until the day of Christ Jesus (Philippians 1:6).

Who began the good work? Jesus. How did He do it? Through the Holy Spirit. We talk about building churches, but we do not build churches because Jesus said, *I will build My church* (Matthew 16:18). Paul said, "Since He's the One who began it, I know He's the One who's going to finish it."

Everything we start will not be finished.

How did we get saved? Did we think it was our idea? THERE IS NONE WHO UNDERSTANDS, THERE IS NONE WHO SEEKS FOR GOD (Romans 3:11). No, not one. *We love, because he first loved us* (1 John 4:19). He chose us. We were chosen by the Spirit, convicted by the Spirit, converted by the Spirit, and will be completed by the Spirit.

Everything we start will not be finished. Everything is winding down to the grave. However, the Apostle Paul said he was *confident of this very thing, that He who began a good work in you will perfect it until the day of Christ Jesus* (Philippians 1:6). No business lasts forever, but anything that God does lasts forever.

Whatever we plan to finish, we need to get started today. Whoever we plan to win to the Lord, we need to get motivated today. Soon and very soon Christ is coming back for His Church.

One day the family of God will gather around the Lord's table, and time will cease to exist as eternity rolls on. The family of God was supernaturally formed and has a sacred fellowship and a secure future!

2

SERVANTS AND SAINTS

About ten years after the Apostle Paul founded the church in Philippi out of a nucleus of people he had won to Christ, he wrote a letter back to them using the form of letter writing that was customary in those days. When we write a letter, we normally begin with a salutation of "Dear So-and-So" followed by the body of the letter and conclude with a complimentary closing such as "Yours truly" or "Cordially yours."

During New Testament times, a little different format was used. The letter began by stating who was writing the letter and to whom the letter was written followed by the body of the letter. Paul used this format in his letter to the Philippians.

Paul wrote from prison stating that *my imprisonment in the cause of Christ has become well known throughout the whole praetorian guard and to everyone else* (Philippians 1:13). In other words, "I am in bonds." Though the man of God can be bound, the Word of God cannot. In addition to the Book of Philippians and the Book of Revelation which was written from the Island of

Patmos by John, the apostle, some of the greatest books of literature have been written from prison cells as well; books such as *The Travels of Marco Polo* and *Pilgrim's Progress* by John Bunyan.

Philippians was also a love letter—a pastor's love letter to his favorite church. Anyone who has ever received a love letter treasures it as did the group of people in Philippi to whom Paul wrote.

WE NEED TO LEAD AS SERVANTS.

Paul opened the letter with, *Paul and Timothy, bond-servants of Christ Jesus* (Philippians 1:1). Paul wrote about half of the books of the New Testament, and Timothy was the young man he led to the Lord on his second missionary journey (Acts 16) who became his traveling companion.

All of God's people are important and of value in the work of the Lord.

Their ages were different with Paul being the older and Timothy the younger. Their experience was different as well as their personalities yet they became one as servants of the Lord, fellow believers in Christ. Their becoming a team shows there are no generation gaps in the Christian faith. All of God's people are important and of value in the work of the Lord.

Paul was the mentor and Timothy the young convert. Every Paul needs a Timothy meaning that every believer needs to win someone to the Lord and then mentor and help them grow and mature in Christ.

Every Timothy needs a Paul meaning every young convert needs an older, mature Christian to take an interest in them. The **who** of the letter are Paul and Timothy.

The **what** of the letter is that they are *bond-servants of Christ Jesus*. This particular statement does not impact us as it would have the original readers. The people of the church at Philippi had gathered together for worship, and Paul had sent his love letter which was being read to them. First they heard the words, *Paul and Timothy*, followed by *bond-servants of Christ Jesus*.

There are two types of slaves in the world: slaves to sin and slaves to Jesus Christ.

This statement would have immediately connected with the people because many of the young Christians in Philippi were slaves. A large percentage of the population in the Roman world was made up of slaves—those who were actually owned by others, bound to someone else. The picture that is drawn from the Roman world is now used to teach a spiritual truth. There are two types of slaves in the world: slaves to sin and slaves to Jesus Christ.

Do you not know that when you present yourselves to someone as slaves for obedience, you are slaves of the one whom you obey? (Romans 6:16). You are a slave to whomever you obey or whatever has you bound. *Jesus answered them, "Truly, truly, I say to you, everyone who commits sin is the slave of sin"* (John 8:34). Sin is addictive and eventually becomes bondage and slavery. There are those who are slaves to drugs, alcohol, their desires, or their jobs. It does not start off that way. A man has a social drink; but before long, the drink has him and he becomes a slave to it. It becomes a terrible bondage.

Do you not know that your body is a temple of the Holy Spirit who is in you, whom you have from God, and that you are not your own? (1 Corinthians 6:19). Those who have received the Lord Jesus as their Savior are now bond slaves of Jesus.

Two pictures illustrate *bond-servants of Christ Jesus.* Slavery in the New Testament meant **ownership**. One person actually owning another person. When a person comes to the Lord Jesus Christ, they are no longer their own. They belong to Christ. He is their master. Every day of their lives, they should wake up and say, "Good morning, Lord. I'm reporting for duty."

Slavery in the New Testament also meant **obedience**. A slave did not plan his own day. Whatever the master commanded was exactly what the slave had to do. When we come to know the Lord Jesus Christ, we learn that He has a plan and a purpose for our lives. The greatest joy we will ever experience is to follow the game plan of Jesus Christ and be obedient to Him.

In regard to slavery in the Old Testament, an owner could keep a slave for six years; but on the seventh year, the slave would be set free. However, in Exodus 21:1-11, we find the scenario of a man who was a slave but was owned by a master who was very kind, generous, and benevolent. This slave was well taken care of and had sufficient food, clothing, and accommodations. If the slave decided that he loved his master and did not want to be set free, his master would bore a hole in the slave's ear which was a symbol that the slave had sold himself for life to his master.

Thankfully, when we give ourselves completely to Christ, we did not receive a hole in our ear; but we do have Jesus in our hearts and are his slaves forever—just as Paul and Timothy were.

WE NEED TO LIVE AS SAINTS.

To all the saints in Christ Jesus (Philippians 1:1). Paul was writing it to all the saints—not just those who have lived especially holy lives. He was writing to Saint Lydia, the business woman who got saved. He was writing to Saint Slave Girl who got saved. He was writing to Saint Jailer who got saved. He was writing *to all the saints in Christ Jesus* in Philippi.

We rarely use the word "saint" these days, but a saint is a saved sinner—one who has been set apart unto Jesus. There are only two kinds of people in the world: the saints and the ain'ts. We are either a saint or we are an ain't.

This is a positional truth—one having to do with our position. For example, if we were to ask a high school student, "What grade are you in?" they might say, "I'm a senior." Their answer is a statement of their position in school. It does not necessarily mean they are "A" students—only that they are seniors in high school. If we are saved, it speaks to our position.

We are either a saint or we are an ain't.

We could ask a college guy, "Are you on the football team?" If he says, "Yes," we could then ask, "What's your position?" "I'm the quarterback." All that says is just what their position on the football team is—not whether they are third string or first string or whether they are All-American and going to be a number 1 pick in the draft.

To all the saints. It is about position, not practice. Ponder this truth. We are saints once we have come to know Christ. We are saints, not because of what we do but because of what Jesus did for us on the cross of Calvary. Someone may ask, "Doesn't it matter how we live?" Just because it has nothing to do with our practice does not mean our practice is unimportant. *But immorality or any impurity or greed must not even be named among you, as is proper among saints* (Ephesians 5:3). Our behavior must be consistent with our position in the Lord.

One of the real problems we are dealing with in the twenty-first century church is that we have a lot of the saints of the Lord who somehow do not understand that just because they are saved, belong to, and have been set apart for the Lord Jesus Christ, they are now to live a different kind of life. If God's people would begin to live up to the level of their sainthood, they would have more impact on a lost and dying world that needs Jesus as their Savior.

To all the saints in Christ Jesus who are in Philippi (Philippians 1:10). Philippi was a strategic city and the physical address of the saints there. However, by including the words, *in Christ Jesus*, Paul also made it their spiritual address. It is the same for those of us who are *in Christ Jesus*. One of Paul's favorite phrases was *in Christ*.

We are in one of two locations: in sin or in Christ. *For as in Adam all die, so also in Christ all will be made alive* (1 Corinthians 15:22). By virtue of our physical birth, we are in the human family—Adam's family; but by virtue of a spiritual birth, we become a part of Jesus's family.

It is not as important where we are as it is whom we are in. Christ is the sphere of our existence. To be in Christ means to be like a fish in water or a bird in the air or a tree in the soil. It describes our spiritual atmosphere—our spiritual address. We have a new address in the Lord Jesus Christ.

Paul's salutation was *grace to you and peace from God our Father and the Lord Jesus Christ* (Philippians 1:2). Paul had a way, through the Holy Spirit, of taking words and exalting and elevating them and filling them with new meaning. It is the way the Lord does with us and in our lives. He takes us and elevates us and fills our life with new meaning.

The Greek word for *grace* is "charis." If we were walking on the streets of Athens, Greece, and saw a friend, we might throw up our hand and say to them, "Charis." If we were in Jerusalem, the word of greeting would be the word *peace*—"shalom" in Hebrew and "eirene" in Greek. Paul takes those two words and fills them with Christian meaning as grace and peace describe the Christian life.

Charis and Eirene are also words commonly used as names for girls—Charis for Karen (or Grace) and Eirene for Irene (or Peace). Karen and Irene—Grace and Peace: twin sisters of the gospel. They can be found together in the Bible. They describe how the Christian life begins, how the Christian life continues, and how the Christian life concludes. Grace and peace always go together.

The Christian life begins with grace—God's unmerited favor. We do not deserve it and cannot earn it yet God sent His Son Jesus to die on the cross to make it possible for us to be forgiven of our sins and receive eternal life. *For by grace you have been saved through faith; and that not of yourselves, it is the gift of God* (Ephesians 2:8). When we are saved by grace, peace enters in.

When we are saved by grace, peace enters in.

So many desire peace but can never find it. They must discover that it is always grace first followed by peace. The order is never reversed. Grace comes walking in the door first every time; but the moment Karen comes in, Irene follows.

Therefore, having been justified by faith, we have peace with God through our Lord Jesus Christ (Romans 5:1). People are desperately looking for that peace of heart, that contentment down deep in their souls, that which they can only find when they accept Jesus Christ as their Lord and Savior.

Paul also wrote about how the Christian life continues. We must have a fresh supply of grace and peace every day. We must have sustaining grace.

If we are dealing with a problem and do not know how to work through it, we must *let the word of Christ richly dwell within [us], with all wisdom teaching and admonishing one another with psalms and hymns and spiritual songs, singing with thankfulness in [our] hearts to God* (Colossians 3:16). God will give us the grace to sing in the hard times.

When temptations come, we must *be strong in the grace that is in Christ Jesus* (2 Timothy 2:1). God can give us that strengthening grace.

We are going to need God's grace and peace when we come to the end of the road, and we know that His *grace is sufficient* (2 Corinthians 12:9). In the moment of death, God will give us dying grace.

Jesus has cornered the market on grace and peace.

Grace and peace. We want it, but where are we going to get it? We cannot go to the hardware store and say, "Give me a gallon of grace and a half a gallon of peace." We cannot go to Walmart and say, "I want two yards of grace and a yard of peace." We cannot go to a bar and say, "Give me a fifth of grace and a fifth of peace." Absolutely not. There is only one place we can find it: *Grace to you and peace from God our Father and the Lord Jesus Christ* (Philippians 1:2).

Jesus has cornered the market on grace and peace. He has a monopoly on the product; but if we want it, He is giving it away to everyone who accepts Him into their hearts.

3

JOYFUL HEART SURGERY

The church in Philippi was greatly involved in the ministry of Paul because they loved him and believed in what he was doing. He had begun the church ten years earlier; and in reading his beautiful letter to them, it is easy to believe that Philippi was the most beloved and favorite of all of the churches he founded.

In his letter, Paul talked about his *imprisonment* (Philippians 1:7,13). Had I been writing a letter from a Philippian jail, it would have been all about **ME**. I would have talked about how uncomfortable it was and how long the chain was that bound me. I would have mentioned how cramped I was and how bad the meals were. However, Paul's letter was all about those who were in the church in Philippi.

Paul told them he thanked *God in all my remembrance of you* (Philippians 1:3) and was *offering prayer with joy in my every prayer for you all* (Philippians 1:4). Paul used the phrase *with joy* regarding his prayer for them. In the previous chapter, Grace and Peace were mentioned as the twin sisters of the gospel with Karen being the name for Grace and Irene being the name for Peace. Grace and Peace go together in the Christian life. However, Grace and Peace have a little sister whose name is Joy. Consequently, when Grace and Peace show up, their sister Joy will invariably come with them.

When Grace and Peace show up, their sister Joy will invariably come with them.

The word "joy" is a key word in Philippians; and even though Paul mentioned it 18 times throughout his letter, he never gave a definition. What he did instead was to give a demonstration of the emotion of joy. Though Paul was in jail and would eventually be beheaded, he could hardly write a sentence without referencing joy. He was a man of joy because his thoughts were filled not with himself but with other people.

Many years ago, someone used the word JOY as an acronym: J–Jesus first; O–others second, and Y–yourself last. When we put Jesus first in our life, others second in our life, and ourselves third, we have found the secret of joy.

Paul makes three basic statements:

1. "I have you in my mind."
2. "I thank my God upon every remembrance of you."
3. "I offer prayer for you with joy."

He was thinking about them and remembering them. They were in his memory bank; and every time he thought of them, his heart was filled with joy.

What do others think when our name is mentioned? What kind of emotions do they feel in their hearts and minds? When they pray for us, is it an occasion of joy or do they do it with tears of grief and anxiety and heartache?

Be anxious for nothing, but in everything by prayer and supplication with thanksgiving let your requests be made known to God (Philippians 4:6). This is what prayer is: asking God. Jesus taught us to *Ask, and it will be given to you; seek, and you will find; knock, and it will be opened to you* (Matthew 7:7).

Paul had a spiritual heart; and as Paul's heart was, so ours ought to be also.

Not only did Paul tell them they were in his mind and in his prayer with joy, but he also told them, *I have you in my heart* (Philippians 1:7).

Sometimes people get on our nerves and can be a "pain in the neck." Some can also give us ulcers because they make us sick to our stomach when we think about them.

When the high priest of the Old Testament would go into the Holy of Holies, he had a breast plate that had 12 beautiful stones on it. On that breast plate was engraved the names of the tribes of the children of Israel symbolizing that when the high priest went into the presence of God, he went with the names of God's people over his heart.

Paul had a spiritual heart; and as Paul's heart was, so ours ought to be also.

WE CAN HAVE THE COMFORT OF COMMUNION.

When we open up Paul's heart, we find the joy of communion. *In view of your participation in the gospel from the first day until now . . .* (Philippians 1:5). The word "communion" can also be used for the word *participation*. "Your communion, your *participation* in the gospel from the first day until now."

Over and over again, Paul referred to the Lord Jesus Christ and the gospel in Philippians 1. Three phrases of note are:

Verse 5: He wrote about their communion (or *participation*) in the gospel (or *fellowship* in the KJV).

1. Verse 12: He wrote about the furtherance (or *greater progress*) of the gospel.
2. Verse 27: He wrote about *striving together for the faith* of the gospel.

Jesus turns friendship into fellowship!

Paul started off with the fellowship of the gospel ("koinonia" in the Greek) which literally means "to have in common"—to be interested in the same things that someone else is interested in. However, Paul was talking about fellowship on a spiritual plane: *If there is any fellowship of the Spirit* (Philippians 2:1)—something spiritual that brings people together. Paul was explaining that when we receive Jesus as our Lord and Savior, we are born into the family of God. By that new birth experience, we are brought into fellowship with the Lord Jesus Christ.

God is faithful, through whom you were called into fellowship with His Son, Jesus Christ our Lord (1 Corinthians 1:9). When we are saved, we are brought into fellowship with Jesus Christ. We now have communion and a relationship with Jesus Christ. However, that is not all. When we come to the Lord, we are not only brought into fellowship with Jesus but also into fellowship with every born-again believer.

What we have seen and heard we proclaim to you also, so that you too may have fellowship with us; and indeed our fellowship is with the Father, and with His Son Jesus Christ (1 John 1:3). When we are saved, we are brought into fellowship with Jesus and with all the brothers and sisters in Jesus. We may have a friendship with someone who does not know Christ as their Savior, but we cannot have fellowship with them. Jesus turns friendship into fellowship!

You all are partakers of grace with me (Philippians 1:7). We are *partakers* when we are in fellowship and have fellowship in grace. When we come to the Lord, we are now a partner in grace with the people of God.

WE CAN HAVE THE CONFIDENCE OF COMPLETION.

We observe something else in Paul's heart: the assurance of completion, an assurance that has to do with God's great work of salvation in our hearts. *For I am confident of this very thing, that He who began a good work in you will perfect it until the day of Christ Jesus* (Philippians 1:6); that is, will finish it *until the day of Christ Jesus*.

When Paul talked about *a good work*, he was talking about God's good work of salvation. He was assured that this great work of salvation which God has begun in our lives, He will carry to completion, that the day of salvation is the guarantee of the day of completion.

There are three days mentioned in Philippians 1:5-6. *From the first day until now* is the present day—the day they got saved, the day they met Jesus.

Lydia, the slave girl, and the jailer were probably sitting in the congregation when this letter was read. Paul told them, "I remember the first day when you came to Jesus." Perhaps Lydia was sitting there thinking, "I remember the first day too. I was out at the riverside prayer meeting when Paul opened up the Scriptures and the Lord opened up my heart. I got saved that day. Yes, I remember the first day."

Perhaps the slave girl thought, "I remember that first day. I was demon-possessed and running after Paul. He turned and rebuked the demons, and the demons came out and Jesus came in. Yes, I remember the first day."

The jailer was perhaps thinking, "I remember the first day. It was at night. I was right on the verge of suicide. I thought all of the prisoners had escaped because of the earthquake. I was getting ready to put a sword in my heart. I got saved. I remember that day quite well."

Do we remember the first day—the day when we came to Jesus? I remember it well. I was saved on a Sunday morning in Montgomery, Alabama. I asked the Lord Jesus to forgive me of my sins and come into my heart and save me. Perhaps others were in their homes or offices or work places when someone came and introduced them to Jesus and that was their first day. *From the first day until now.*

For I am confident of this very thing, that He who began a good work in you will perfect it until the day of Christ Jesus (Philippians 1:6). *For by grace you have been saved through faith; and that not of yourselves, it is the gift of God* (Ephesians 2:8). *For we are His workmanship* (Ephesians 2:10).

Salvation is not because of our works. It is because of His good work; salvation is of the Lord. He initiates it. When it comes to our salvation, God thought it, Jesus bought it, the Holy Spirit wrought it, the devil fought it; but praise God, we got it!

Not only does Paul talk about the initiation of the good work but also about the location of the good work. Where is God doing this good work of salvation? *For I am confident of this very thing, that He who began a good work **IN YOU*** (Philippians 1:6 Emphasis added). He is doing His good work of salvation in believers.

Someone once said, "Let's just find where God is working and get in on it." However, we know that God is working in the hearts and lives of people everywhere in the world. It is an inside job.

We are all under construction for God is doing a work in our lives. *We are His workmanship* (Ephesians 2:10). This is where we get our word poem—God's poem. The picture is like a diamond in the rough. When a diamond is discovered, it is taken and cleaned and polished and shaped. God is doing a good work in us, but what exactly? What is God's purpose? *For those whom He foreknew, He also predestined to become conformed to the image of His Son* (Romans 8:29). He is making us like Jesus. Sometimes we may think, "God isn't doing too well because I'm not a whole lot like Jesus"; but ultimately, God is going to make us to be like Jesus.

When it comes to our salvation, God thought it, Jesus bought it, the Holy Spirit wrought it, the devil fought it; but praise God, we got it!

A sculptor once had a big chunk of marble and began chiseling it. Someone came by and asked what he was doing; and he said, "I'm chiseling a horse." The man looked at the chunk of marble and said, "You're chiseling a horse? I don't see a horse there. How are you chiseling a horse out of that big chunk of marble?" The sculptor said, "It's really easy. I just chip away everything that doesn't look like a horse."

There are things in our lives that are not like Jesus so God just continues to chip away at them; and one of these days, everything superfluous is going to be chipped away and we will be found to be in the image of His son.

For I am confident of this very thing, that He who began a good work in you will perfect it until the day of Christ Jesus (Philippians 1:6). That is the completion of God's good work: *the day of Jesus Christ.* We will be the accomplishment of His good work. God never started a project He did not finish. We cannot say that about our government because there are many things they have begun but never finished. However, God has completed every project He ever started.

It was true of creation. *Thus the heavens and the earth were completed* (Genesis 2:1). He started His creation work; He finished His creation work. The same is true about the work of redemption that Jesus did on the cross. On the cross, Jesus proclaimed, *It is finished!* (John 19:30). He finished the work of redemption to make our salvation possible.

Love is sometimes painful.

One of these days God has said that the good work He has started in us, He will finish. We are going to be like Christ and with Him in heaven forever.

WE CAN HAVE THE CONSCIOUSNESS OF COMPASSION.

When we open Paul's heart, we see communion and confidence. We have seen the joy of communion and fellowship in the gospel. Afterwards, Paul gave us the warmth of compassion.

For God is my record, how greatly I long after you all in the bowels of Jesus Christ (Philippians 1:8 KJV). Paul had a compassion for these people which was deeply emotional. When he said, *how I long after you all*, it means to pursue, to go all out. It is an all-out kind of love.

Love is a decision. Many people who get married think love is just an emotion, saying, "I fell in love" or "It was just puppy love." It is best to be careful with puppy love—it could lead to a dog's life.

How greatly I long after you all in the bowels of Jesus Christ. Why did the King James Version translate it as the bowels of Jesus Christ? Because that is the exact meaning of the Greek word. The Greeks believed that the seat of the emotions was in the inner organs.

People used to laugh at the very idea that our emotions affect our inner organs or that our inner organs affect our emotions. We do not laugh anymore because we know it is true. Perhaps that is where the song, "I Love You So Much It Hurts," by Floyd Tillman got its inspiration. Love is sometimes painful.

The first mile is a trial, but the second mile is a smile!

Love affects the organs in our bodies and can cause ulcers. Love means inner affections. "I love you with inner affections." It is an emotional thing, and that is the way we should love our brothers and sisters in the Lord. That is also the way we should love lost people. It should be an emotional thing.

Not only is it an emotional thing, but it is also a supernatural thing. Paul was very careful in his language. He did not say, "I love you with my affections," but "I long for you all in the affections"—not Paul's affections but the affections of Jesus Christ. We are doing spiritual heart surgery on Paul. When we open his spiritual heart, we make a startling discovery. There is another heart in there—the heart of Jesus Christ. "I long after you all in the tender affections of Jesus Christ."

We can attempt to love people every day of our lives; however, we will eventually come to the realization that we cannot really love people without "the affections of Christ."

On one occasion, Jesus said, *whoever slaps you on your right cheek, turn the other to him also. If anyone wants to sue you and take your shirt, let him have your coat also. Whoever forces you to go one mile, go with him two* (Matthew 5:39-41). We cannot achieve this in our own strength; it is a supernatural thing. We are to love people with the affections of Christ. The first mile is a trial, but the second mile is a smile!

4

THE HALLELUJAH PRAYER!

And this I pray (Philippians 1:9). Prayer is a vital part of the Christian life; and as believers, we must become men and women of prayer because prayer is the lifeline between us and heaven. It is the communication system that keeps us in contact with God.

There are no Ph.D. degrees in prayer. The disciples said to Jesus, *Lord, teach us to pray* (Luke 11:1). That is an interesting statement in that they did not say, "Lord, teach us to preach," or "Lord, teach us how to perform miracles." In time, the disciples did perform miracles, but their desire was for the Lord to teach them to pray.

If we pray better, we will live better; and if we pray more, we will have more joy. Paul said, *Always offering prayer with joy in my every prayer for you all* (Philippians 1:4). Prayer and joy go together; prayerful people are happier people. Prayer transforms burdens into blessings, pains into praise, and griefs into glory. When we go to our knees in prayer with heavy burdens and sorrows in our hearts, God transforms those heartaches into glory hallelujahs.

Prayer transforms burdens into blessings, pains into praise, and griefs into glory.

There are numerous written prayers of Paul interspersed in his writings, and the Holy Spirit has made them part of Scripture as illustrations and guidelines to us as to what prayer is all about and how to have our prayers answered.

Paul takes us into his prayer closet—a sacred place. He shows us the kinds of things he prayed for while he was in prison. The secret of our success or failure as Christians will be found in the prayer closet. We are no better than our prayers.

WE NEED TO INCORPORATE THE FOUNDATION OF PRAYER.

It is vital that we learn to pray. There are several matters concerning prayer that are apparent in Philippians.

Prayer is a **personal matter** as revealed in Paul's statement, *And this I pray*. Paul was a Pharisee before his conversion; and as thus, he was probably one of those who would stand on a street corner and pray . . . first being certain that he had an audience. He would have prayed in order to impress other people around him as to what a religious person he was. Do we pray prayers or do we say prayers?

Then Paul met Jesus on the Damascus Road. After three days, the Lord spoke to Ananias saying, *Get up . . . and inquire at the house of Judas for a man from Tarsus named Saul, for he is praying* (Acts 9:11). Paul became a praying man. If we are genuinely born-again believers in Jesus, we pray also. Statistics reflect that the majority of people in America pray, but do they pray prayers or just say prayers?

A prayerless soul is a Christless soul. If we never pray, how can we truly have Jesus as our personal Savior. Prayer is personal—something that no one can do for you. Others can make intercession for us, but they cannot pray the prayer that we are supposed to pray for ourselves. We are the only one who can truly pray the prayers that we need to pray unto the Lord.

A prayer in general never hits anything in particular.

Prayer is **powerful**. When Paul was writing the letter to the Philippians, he was in jail with chains on his hands as well as his feet. He knelt on a slimy floor in a vermin-filled Roman prison and lifted his chained hands toward heaven. When he did, he unleashed a power greater than the power of the Roman legions that marched throughout the entire empire. Satan laughs at our works and mocks our thinking, but he trembles at our prayers.

Prayer is **purposeful**. Prayer has a sense of direction to it. A prayer in general never hits anything in particular; therefore, we must learn to focus our prayers—to get laser-beam sharp being very specific and direct.

For example, when we pray for the lost, what do we pray? For all of the lost people in the world? That a wonderful thing to do, but how about focusing that prayer on some lost person we know by name. Do we use a prayer list? Paul did. As we read the letters of Paul, we find that he mentions numerous people. Do we write down the names of people we are praying for or the various situations we are praying for? If we do not have a list, how will we know when God answers a prayer if we do not know what we have prayed for or what we are praying for?

WE NEED TO INCLUDE THE FORMULA OF PRAYER.

What was Paul praying for in particular? If we were in jail with conditions as bad as they say they were in that day, I can imagine that a whole lot of our praying would be, "Oh, Lord! Please get me out of this miserable place. I can't stand it much longer. The food is awful. Please get me out where I can at least have a good meal at McDonald's. Help me!"

However, Paul prayed, *And this I pray, that your love may abound still more and more in real knowledge and all discernment, so that you may approve the things that are excellent, in order to be sincere and blameless until the day of Christ* (Philippians 1:9-10). He was praying for them.

One of the great privileges we have is the privilege of praying for other people. It means so much when someone tells us, "I'm praying for you," or when we receive a text or email stating, "I want you to know I am praying for you." It is not only a privilege to know that someone is praying for us but also a privilege for us to be able to pray for someone else.

Although there is a time and a place when we pray for ourselves, Paul was not praying for himself. Rather, he was praying for others and being very specific in his prayers. In this instance, Paul's prayer was elevated by the Holy Spirit so that his prayer not only went to the Philippian believers of that day but is also available now to all believers everywhere. The things Paul prayed for them are the things that we should pray for now.

And this I pray, that your love may abound still more and more in real knowledge and all discernment (Philippians 1:9). Paul was praying that they would be **growing Christians**.

When we receive Christ as our personal Savior, *the love of God has been poured out within our hearts through the Holy Spirit who was given to us* (Romans 5:5). If we know Christ as our Savior, God will teach us how to love.

Paul was praying that our love would be a growing experience. He pictured love like an overflowing stream, a bubbling fountain, a flowing river. He was saying, "I am praying that your love may abound more and more." A believer once prayed, "Lord, we can't hold much, but we can overflow a lot." How true.

God can help us grow in our love for Jesus, for other Christians, and for lost people. He is saying, "I want your love to abound, to flow over more and more." However, He puts some banks on the river of love. He wants our love to abound *more and more in real knowledge and all discernment* (Philippians 1:9). Knowledge and discernment are the two banks of the river love because if a river gets out of its banks, it can be very destructive as we see when floods come.

Knowledge and discernment are the two banks of the river love.

On the one hand, we need knowledge. We must study our Bibles and know how to pray and love people. On the other hand, we need discernment—insight and understanding.

We learn from the Lord that we are to love and then use that love and channel it in the right direction. For example, a little child who loves cats has an inclination to reach out and put its arms around one. However, tigers are in the cat family also. We must learn to use discernment and keep love within its proper bounds. The Lord would have us pray that we would be growing Christians.

Paul was also praying that they would be **genuine Christians**. He wanted them to be the "real deal" *so that you may approve the things that are excellent, in order to be sincere and blameless until the day of Christ* (Philippians 1:10). *Approve the things that are excellent* means to put to the test the things that are different. We must be genuine in our choices in life.

Life is a series of choices and not all things are equal. Paul was saying, "I'm praying that you will try the things that are different, that you will put them to the test so that you will be able to approve the best things and discard those things that are not the best." God wants us to learn to make a differentiation between the bad and the good, the good and the better, and the better and the best.

Sometimes we are wrapped up with things that do not matter. At times, our sense of values is out of perspective, and we lose a sense of balance. In our American culture, we have lost our sense of values. Christians in poverty-stricken nations often get more done with less. We have more but do little; they have little but do more. We pay our entertainers and sports personalities millions of dollars each year while our missionaries risk everything for the gospel and get paid very little. Something is not right there. We have not learned to put to the test the things that matter the most.

The same measurement is true in our lives. We need to learn to be discerning in our day-to-day lives. There are books that are simply not worth reading yet we continue to fill our minds with them. There are places that are simply not worth going to yet we continue to go. There are activities that simply waste our time yet we continue to participate in them. As Christians, we must learn to be genuine in our choices and choose the best and most important things in life.

Paul tells us to be sincere and genuine in our character. The English word sincere comes from the Latin word sincerus, meaning whole, clean, pure, genuine, truthful.

The Greek word for sincere means frank, outspoken, candid, forthright, open. The word is derived from heile (the sun's ray) and krino and means tested as genuine or pure. It literally means to examine by the sunlight. In other words, we could take a porcelain vase and lift it to the sunlight. If there was a flaw in the vase, the sunlight would reveal that it was not pure piece.

This is what God is praying for us—to be genuine Christians whose lives can be examined by the sunlight of the Lord and that God will look at us and see that we are the "real deal." Jesus said that *he who practices the truth comes to the Light* (John 3:21). If our lives are genuine and sincere, we will not mind when the light is turned upon us.

Without offence (Philippians 1:10 KJV) means to give no cause for stumbling. Our prayer is that there would be nothing in our lives that would cause anyone to stumble. "My prayer for you is that you would be sincere, examined by the sunlight, without offense, having nothing in your life that would cause someone to stumble or be hindered, until the day of Jesus Christ."

Paul reminds us we should be living with our eyes on the coming of the Lord Jesus. We should live in a manner that if Jesus were to come today, we would say, "Welcome, Jesus. I've been waiting for You. I've been living for You, Lord."

God wants us to be growing Christians *that [our] love may abound* (Philippians 1:9) and genuine Christians, *sincere and blameless until the day of Christ* (Philippians 1:10).

Paul also wants us to be **good Christians**, *having been filled with the fruit of righteousness which comes through Jesus Christ* (Philippians 1:11). The picture is of a fruit tree, and Paul compares the Christian to a tree that is bearing fruit. Our lives will begin to demonstrate the good things that come when Christ lives in us. What is inside us will ultimately determine what comes out in our daily lives. Hopefully, we will be fruit-bearing Christians.

Abide in Me, and I in you. As the branch cannot bear fruit of itself unless it abides in the vine, so neither can you unless you abide in Me (John 15:4). How do we bear fruit and fruit that remains? Jesus said, *Abide in Me*. When we abide in Jesus and stay in fellowship with Him, then Jesus on the inside can begin to produce fruit on the outside. This is the essence of being a good Christian.

WE NEED TO BE INSPIRED WITH THE FAITH OF PRAYER.

Regarding the dynamics of prayer, Paul uses the words, *to the glory and praise of God* (Philippians 1:11). The goal of prayer is to be *to the glory and praise of God*. God prays for us that our lives might be to the glory and praise of God. He is praying that we will be inspired by the **goal of prayer**.

Jesus said, *Let your light shine before men in such a way that they may see your good works, and glorify your Father who is in heaven* (Matthew 5:16). If we live and behave the way we should, then God will get the glory. We are to live *to the glory and praise of God* so that God will not only get the attention but also the adoration. People will praise the Lord because of our lives.

Praise without prayer is presumption; however, prayer without praise is ingratitude.

Paul was an incredible prayer warrior and wrapped his prayer up with the **dynamics of prayer**. He prayed *to the glory and praise of God*. Praise is the follow-through of prayer. Praise wraps up our prayer. Praise without prayer is presumption; however, prayer without praise is ingratitude. We should live our lives in such a way as to be a testimony for the Lord Jesus Christ so that God will get the glory and the praise.

There was an amazing Christian lady whose life was such a testimony that when she died, it seemed as if it were just a natural promotion for her into heaven. People wanted to be better people because of her life and wanted to praise the Lord because of her testimony. Her son was a noted and gifted organist and played at his mother's funeral. He put into the music that day all of his emotions, feelings, and gratitude for his sweet, loving, Christian mother. When the service concluded and the casket was being carried up the aisle, the organ burst into a full-throated sound of the "Hallelujah Chorus"!

Our prayer should be that when the time comes for our transition from this world to the heavenly realm, our life will have been *to the glory and praise of God* to the extent that people will say "Hallelujah!"

THE PREACHING OF THE CHRISTIAN LIFE (PHILIPPIANS 1:12-20)

5

TURNING CHAINS INTO GAINS

In Philippians 1:12-20, the Apostle Paul was writing about some of the circumstances of his life in such a manner that it helps us try to get into his shoes and see how he felt and what he was experiencing. His circumstances at this particular time were not exactly appealing. Things were not going well for Paul as a prisoner in a jail cell in Rome.

A variety of misfortunes had come his way. He had been victimized by an illegal trial, arrested, and placed on a ship to Rome. Along the way, there had been a shipwreck; and he had been marooned on an island for a period of time. When he arrived in Rome, he was placed in prison with chains on his wrists and ankles.

In addition to this, the Christian community in Rome was not overly receptive to the Apostle Paul. There were preachers who were jealous of him and rather glad that he was in prison. Consequently, Paul's circumstances were terrible and extremely undesirable.

As Paul dealt with these circumstances, what he did not say and what he did say is very "telling." He used the words, *have turned out* (Philippians 1:12). We know that things do not "just happen" to the people of God. Although many think that life is simply a series of happenstances and that life has no meaning or purpose, those who know the Lord believe something altogether different. The circumstances of our life are not happenstances; they are providences.

The circumstances of our life are not happenstances; they are providences.

God is at work in our lives. We have a loving heavenly Father who takes everything that comes our way and filters it through His will and providence so that it has a divine intention and a divine design. Paul said that things turn out for a divine purpose and reason.

He quickly dismissed all of the circumstances that had happened to him and accepted imprisonment, physical difficulties, and reversals. He frequently made mention of the Lord Jesus and the gospel because his mind was focused on the good news of Jesus and getting the message out to the world.

> *In view of your participation in the gospel from the first day until now* (Philippians 1:5).

> *My circumstances have turned out for the greater progress of the gospel* (Philippians 1:12).

> *Striving together for the faith of the gospel* (Philippians 1:27).

Throughout Paul's writing in Philippians 1, he made mention of Jesus Christ who held first place in his life. His great desire was that the good news of what Jesus had done on the cross of Calvary be known to the whole world, and he admonished them to *conduct yourselves in a manner worthy of the gospel of Christ, so that whether I come and see you or remain absent, I will hear of you that you are standing firm in one spirit, with one mind striving together for the faith of the gospel* (Philippians 1:27).

As Christians, things do not just happen to us. No matter what is happening in our lives, if Jesus is number one and if we are totally focused on proclaiming the good news of Jesus, our circumstances will be turned into opportunities.

WE HAVE OPPORTUNITIES TO EXTEND THE GOSPEL.

The circumstances of our lives are opportunities for the gospel to be extended.

Paul said his circumstances had *turned out for the greater progress of the gospel* (Philippians 1:12). Although Paul was in jail, he knew it was not over. Although he could no longer travel, he knew it was not the end. His opportunities to preach the gospel has not ended but rather, in his circumstances, had been extended.

Paul's words for *the greater progress* in the Greek language literally meant "to cut before." It was used to describe an advanced team of soldiers who would prepare the way for the army that was soon to follow. Paul was saying that "although I am in jail and am no longer able to travel, I want you to know that my circumstances are opportunities for the gospel of Jesus Christ to be advanced." Paul was a spiritual trailblazer for Jesus.

We would be biblically wise to view every circumstance of our lives the way Paul viewed himself and ask ourselves the question, "How can my circumstance advance the gospel?" Unfortunately, we are often content to do the same old things—business as usual.

My imprisonment in the cause of Christ has become well known throughout the whole praetorian guard and to everyone else (Philippians 1:13). Emperor Tiberius built a palace to house the 9,000 soldiers of the Praetorian Guard. They were the best troops of the Roman Empire, akin to our own Special Forces. They were the special bodyguards of the emperor similar to the Swiss Guard at the Vatican.

The circumstances of our lives are opportunities for the gospel to be extended.

Paul was under 24-hour surveillance by members of the Praetorian Guard. Paul would be chained to one of the guards for approximately four hours after which there would be a change. In a 24-hour period of time, there would be six soldiers who would be guarding Paul.

Had I been in Paul's predicament, rather than writing letters of encouragement, I would probably have been writing to family or friends and complaining about how tight the chains were around my wrists, how long or short the chains were on my ankles, how foul the soldiers' language was, and just how generally uncomfortable I was. However, Paul said in his letter, *My circumstances have turned out for the greater progress of the gospel* (Philippians 1:12). Paul saw the soldiers as an opportunity to extend the gospel and tell them about the Lord Jesus Christ.

Imagine the talk that was going on in the Praetorian Guard. "What did you do yesterday?" "I spent four hours chained to a guy named Paul over at the jail." "Who's he?" "A guy from Tarsus." "Why is he in prison?" "They sent him here to go on trial because he believes in somebody named Jesus." "Who's Jesus?" "Paul says Jesus is a Jew who died on a cross and that when He died on the cross, He paid the price for the sins of the whole world." "You don't mean it. That's what the guy said?"

"He did!" "Man, I'm guarding him tomorrow. I'll see what he has to say." Paul was what we might call a "chain preacher."

The Praetorian Guard came and went; and during all that time, Paul was having the opportunity to tell them about Jesus. We know this because Paul wrote, *My imprisonment in the cause of Christ has become well known throughout the whole praetorian guard and to everyone else* (Philippians 1:13). We know his influence extended even into Caesar's household: *All the saints greet you, especially those of Caesar's household* (Philippians 4:22). Because of Paul's circumstances of being chained to the Praetorian Guard and winning them to Christ, they were witnessing to others—all the way up to Caesar's palace. What an opportunity for the gospel to be extended!

There are times in life when we may feel that we are chained to a circumstance we cannot escape. Perhaps it is being chained to a job we dislike or a health issue. Even in those circumstances, God can use us to get the gospel of Jesus Christ to places where it has never been. Perhaps a stay in the hospital is an opportunity to tell a nurse or an intern or a medical doctor about our faith in the Lord Jesus Christ. We need to realize that things do not just "happen" to Christians. If Jesus is first in our life, there will be opportunities for the gospel to be extended.

WE HAVE OPPORTUNITIES TO ENCOURAGE OTHERS.

Paul's arrival in Rome emboldened others to be a witness for the Lord. *Most of the brethren, trusting in the Lord because of my imprisonment, have far more courage to speak the word of God without fear* (Philippians 1:14). When they saw Paul witnessing under adverse circumstances, in jail and facing death, it encouraged some of the more hesitant, timid, and fearful believers in the church in Rome.

Courage begets courage; enthusiasm begets enthusiasm. A bold witness for the Lord may encourage someone else to be a bold witness for Jesus Christ. When one Christian gets on fire and starts witnessing for the Lord, it sparks a fire in the heart of someone else. Paul felt that his witnessing caused others to be a witness.

Courage begets courage; enthusiasm begets enthusiasm.

Paul then pointed out that *some, to be sure, are preaching Christ even from envy and strife but some also from good will; the latter do it out of love, knowing that I am appointed for the defense of the gospel; the former proclaim Christ out of selfish ambition rather than from pure motives, thinking to cause me distress in my imprisonment* (Philippians 1:15-17). When we read about the New Testament churches, we sometimes get the idea that they were perfect, that they never had any problems. If we think the early church was perfect, we are thinking about the church that never was.

When we read the various letters to the New Testament churches, we discover that every problem we have in churches today was found in some form in the early church. The church is made up of people—saved sinners. None is perfect.

Some of the people who were preaching were doing it *out of selfish ambition rather than from pure motives*. They were not sincere and were even glad that Paul was in jail. Paul came to Rome and was in the spotlight so they were not getting the attention they were accustomed to.

Sometimes it is hard for some singers to be blessed when someone else is singing just a little bit better than they sing. Sometimes it is hard for some preachers to be blessed when some other preacher is preaching just a little bit better than they preach. There are some who are witnessing for Jesus out of pure motives and others with impure motives. Though it is possible to serve the Lord with impure motives, we need to be very careful about our own motives.

What was Paul to do? He could have given the Praetorian Guard an earful about how sorry and low-down those so-called "Christians" were. However, had he done that, the angels would have wept and a lost world would have sneered. We must be extremely careful as to how we respond to others, particularly if they respond to us with jealousy and envy.

The closer we get to Jesus, the more we see our own inconsistencies and failures.

George Whitefield (also known as George Whitfield) and John Wesley were contemporaries. Whitefield was somewhat stronger in the doctrines of grace, election, and predestination while Wesley was somewhat stronger in the areas of human responsibility and free will. Consequently, they had some doctrinal disagreements. Someone who knew about their disagreement once asked Mr. Whitefield, "Do you expect to see John Wesley in heaven?" Mr. Whitefield responded, "I do not. I expect Mr. Wesley to be so close to the throne and me so far from the throne that I won't be able to see him at all." That is the kind of response God wants us to have.

Paul responded regarding those with impure motives, *Whether in pretense or in truth, Christ is proclaimed; and in this I rejoice* (Philippians 1:18). It matters not whether anyone does something the way we do it; it matters not who gains the attention. The bottom line is that Jesus Christ is preached and that people come to know our Lord and Savior, Jesus Christ.

Do we rejoice when God blesses the ministry of others? Rather than being bothered by God's blessing someone else's ministry, we should be filled with amazement as to why God blesses our ministry. The closer we get to Jesus, the more we see our own inconsistencies and failures. When we do, we are not going to have a lot of time to sit around passing judgment on the behavior and activities of others because we will be amazed that God ever chose to use us the way He has.

WE HAVE OPPORTUNITIES FOR CHRIST TO BE EXALTED.

As Christians, things do not just happen to us. When Jesus is first in our life, our circumstances are opportunities for the Lord Jesus Christ to be exalted. *For I know that this will turn out for my deliverance* (Philippians 1:19). Paul was not talking about his soul's salvation but about salvaging good out of a bad circumstance. He was talking about God's rescuing what seemed to be an impossible situation. He went on to say that *I know that this will turn out for my deliverance through your prayers and the provision of the Spirit of Jesus Christ* (Philippians 1:19).

Paul was able to deal with these circumstances victoriously because he turned his eyes away from his own circumstances as though they were just passing experiences and had his eyes on something better. *My earnest expectation and hope [is] that I will not be put to shame in anything, but that with all boldness, Christ will even now, as always, be exalted in my body, whether by life or by death* (Philippians 1:20).

When we arrive at the place in our faith where we can say, "I don't care what comes in my life; I just want Jesus to get the honor and the glory, and I want Him to be exalted in my life through this circumstance," then we are on victory ground!

There are two ways to magnify something: with a microscope or a telescope. A microscope takes something small and makes it large. A telescope takes something very distant and brings it near.

Paul says that what we want is for Jesus to be magnified in our body—for our body to be like a microscope to take that which is small and make it big. We are not suggesting that Jesus is small; however, He is small in the lives of many. Paul was saying, "I want my life and my body to be like a microscope in order to take Jesus, who seems to be so unimportant to this world, and make Him large in my life so that others can see Jesus in me."

Paul also says, "I want my life to be like a telescope—to take that which is far and bring it near." This is not to imply that Jesus is distant because He is right here with every one of us. However, to a lot of people He is distant; and by the lens of our life, we want to make Jesus become very near. When people get around us, do they feel like they are in the presence of Jesus? Do they feel like Jesus is near to them?

Whatever our circumstances are, they are opportunities for Jesus to be exalted.

With all boldness, Christ will even now, as always, be exalted in my body, whether by life or by death (Philippians 1:20). By life and by death are the two ultimate circumstances. We are either living or we are dying. This great apostle was saying that whichever of the ultimate circumstances—whether he lived or whether he died—he wanted Jesus to be exalted. May we live so that in whatever circumstances of life we find ourselves, people will see Jesus in us. When we come to the time of death, may we be such a testimony for the Lord that even our dying will be a witness for the Lord. We are to bring honor to Jesus. Whatever our circumstances are, they are opportunities for Jesus to be exalted.

6

THE PARADIGMS OF A PRISONER

For millions of people, there is a pessimism about life and its meaning. The Bible tells of those who wasted their lives with riotous living. Consequently, how refreshing it is to turn to a positive statement from someone who has found real meaning, purpose, and fulfillment in life.

The Apostle Paul gave his amazing philosophy of life in Philippians 1:21. He showed us life's grandest paradigms by which we view life. Down through the years, many students were asked to write their philosophy of life in their high school English class. Paul had figured out his personal philosophy of life and lived it to the extent that he could say, *I have finished the course* (2 Timothy 4:7). In eleven words of one syllable each, he also said, *For to me, to live is Christ and to die is gain* (Philippians 1:21). I have often expressed to my daughters, "The secret to success is to find God's will, follow God's will, and finish God's will." That is the essence of dreaming and then doing what is the most important in life.

It is refreshing to listen to someone who has discovered what life is really about and has found that life can have a God-given purpose. Life can be wonderful, positive, and fulfilling. It is so vital that we not waste our lives but personally cultivate the kind of faith-filled paradigms that will empower our lives for years to come.

The secret to success is to find God's will, follow God's will, and finish God's will.

WE NEED TO DEVELOP A POWERFUL PHILOSOPHY.

Someone once said that life is what a person is alive to. For instance, a husband and wife are at home watching television. While flipping through the cable channels, the husband finds the home channel and his wife comes alive. He continues to channel search and finds a college football game, and he comes alive. Life is what we are alive to.

This same husband and wife go to a department store. As they walk through the store, the wife goes by the dress section and immediately comes alive. They walk a little farther and come to the sporting goods section and the husband immediately comes alive. Life is what we are alive to.

Personally Alive

Paul shared several aspects of his life. He said, *For to me, to live is Christ* (Philippians 1:21). He said that what he was alive to was Jesus Christ. For Paul, Jesus was the basis of life, the beginning of life, the bounty of life, the beauty of life, and the benediction of life. For him, life was wrapped up in one sentence: *For to me, to live is Christ*. Paul believed his life with the Lord Jesus Christ was very **personal** and was expressing how personal the Christian experience was to him. Can we say that about our lives?

Being a Christian is not just a matter of going to church or subscribing to a particular creed. Christianity is a personal relationship with the Lord Jesus Christ. One of the wonderful truths in the Bible is to discover that God is personally interested in each one of us. We are living in a very impersonal world where people are often known by a number rather than by their names. However, the Word of God instructs us that God is interested in us individually. Jesus said, *My sheep hear My voice, and I know them, and they follow Me* (John 10:27). We learn in the Book of Revelation about the antichrist and that those who are his will have the number 666, but God's people do not have numbers. They have names. God knows us, and we are very special to Him.

Practically Alive

Our philosophy should not only be personal but also **practical**. When Paul said, *For to me, to live is Christ*, he was talking about real living. Unfortunately, many people do not really live; they merely exist. They go through life without a complete understanding as to why they are living. Life is a grind. They get up at the same time each morning, eat the same thing for breakfast, get in the same car, go to the same office, and go through the same routine every weekday. As they head for the weekend, they do the same things. For them, living is merely existing—just getting by. It is buying cars and food and having clothing in their closets. This is their concept of what it is to live on this earth.

However, life is not just how many things a person can accumulate or how many "toys" they can acquire. When the Apostle Paul said, *For to me, to live is Christ*, he was saying, "I have found the meaning of existence; I have found the purpose of life. For me, living is Jesus Christ." Many people never understand that their faith in Jesus affects their daily lives. Everything about their life and every aspect of their life should be touched by their relationship with the Lord Jesus Christ.

Paul's philosophy of life was, "It is personal to me. It is practical to live." Not only that, he also said it was possible for us to *live is Christ*.

Presently Alive

It is interesting that Paul used the simple word "is" to illustrate "when" he was in Christ. We know the where because he taught us in Ephesians that we are seated in the heavenlies with Christ. In Philippians, he says for us to live is Christ. He was not planning on living for Christ only when he found the time. For him, Christ was in his every day and his every way. Is Christ as real to us as the book we are now holding in our hand? The book we are holding is not a "was" or a "will" but an "is." A lot of us do not practice the presence of the Lord enough in our lives. Instead of the daily grind, we should experience the daily find! Christ is presently with us, and we can live for Him, with Him, and in Him.

Potentially Alive

Some may be thinking, "I would like to enjoy that kind of experience, but I'm not sure it's possible. I have tried to live the Christian life, and I just can't. I have tried to have joy and peace and meaning in my life, and yet I don't have it. I don't have the power to do it." In actuality, no one has the power to do it either for Paul says, *For to me, to live is Christ*.

When we come to Christ, we can experience *I have been crucified with Christ; and it is no longer I who live, but Christ lives in me; and the life which I now live in the flesh I live by faith in the Son of God, who loved me and gave Himself up for me* (Galatians 2:20). It is our faith in Christ that gives us the power to live the way we should live.

Using a single sentence, develop a philosophy as to why we are on this earth. Let us refine our thoughts and narrow our focus until we can say, *For to me . . .*

I have often been asked how I have maintained my focus over the decades. When I came to Christ at the age of 12, I knew He had a divine purpose for my life. In those early years, I sought His face until I knew His will for my life. Knowing the "why" changed everything and brought focus for years to come.

Instead of the daily grind, we should experience the daily find!

When I entered the University of South Alabama in Mobile, I only took courses that I knew would transfer to Central Bible College where I planned to focus on a BA in Bible. When I finally arrived at CBC, every single college hour I had taken at USA was credited to my account. On my first day of class, I knew I was only passing through to what the Lord had for me to do in this life. Eighteen months later, I walked the graduation line and moved on to work on an MA in Bible, an MDiv in Pastoral Leadership at the Assemblies of God Theological Seminary, and a DMin in Preaching at Trinity Evangelical Divinity School.

While I was progressing through my study years, I was also developing my preaching ministry at the same time. When I was 23 and in my first year at the Assemblies of God Theological Seminary, I developed a mission statement and launched a nonprofit, Cutting Edge International.

The purpose of Cutting Edge International is to fulfill the Great Commission that Jesus Christ gave to His disciples (Matthew 28:18-20). Cutting Edge International seeks to fulfill the three-fold demand of the Great Commission. First, it seeks to evangelize the world with Christ's power (Mathew 28:18). Second, it seeks to evangelize the world with Christ's program (Mathew 28:19-20a). Third, it seeks to evangelize the world with Christ's presence (Matthew 28:20b).

This Christ-centered "why" has eliminated the unnecessary from my life. For me, every day is *For to me, to live is Christ.* If there is anything more important than this, I do not know what it is.

This Christ-centered "why" has eliminated the unnecessary from my life.

During those early years, I preached on the weekends, ministered in youth rallies on Mondays, and began preaching at youth camps during the summer. During my first semester, I remember saying to my dormmate, "I plan to do a lot of preaching while I am at CBC." He responded, "You will not do much preaching because there are hundreds of preachers in this area. Why would you think you will be preaching a lot?" I answered, "Because I am willing to preach anywhere. If you are willing to preach anywhere, there will always be a place for you to preach."

Being willing to preach anywhere at any time is a powerful philosophy of life. I would challenge each person to captivate their own "why" and get started with their own divine purpose.

WE NEED A PRODUCTIVE PERSONHOOD.

Keeping in mind that Paul was writing this letter to the believers in the church of Philippi, we need to realize that, in addition to founding this church, he also won many of those people to faith in the Lord Jesus Christ. He had concluded that he was not going to die but was going to live. As he reflected on living, he looked at the whole idea of his purpose. Through Paul's ministry, we learn what quality of life really means and how to have purpose and meaning in life.

Indispensable

But if I am to live on in the flesh, this will mean fruitful labor (Philippians 1:22). *Yet to remain on in the flesh is more necessary for your sake* (Philippians 1:24). Paul was talking about the ministry he was going to have with the people at the church at Philippi and was convinced that his ministry was going to be needful to them.

One of the ways people grow and mature in their Christian life is by mentoring others.

We must take note of the focus of Paul's life. He was not focusing on himself but on other people. In Philippians 1:24-26, he uses the words "you" or "your" five times. He was living for the benefit of others—not living his life to satisfy himself.

> *²⁴Yet to remain on in the flesh is more necessary for your sake. ²⁵Convinced of this, I know that I will remain and continue with you all for your progress and joy in the faith, ²⁶so that your proud confidence in me may abound in Christ Jesus through my coming to you again.*

The King James version of Philippians 1:25 uses the word, "furtherance": *And having this confidence, I know that I shall abide and continue with you all for your furtherance and joy of faith.*

In Philippians 1:12 (KJV), Paul also writes about the furtherance of the gospel. *But I would ye should understand, brethren, that the things which happened unto me have fallen out rather unto the furtherance of the gospel.* Furtherance means to cut in advance, to go before, to cut before. It is the picture of advancement, of progress.

Paul was telling them that "I am convinced that my ministry is needful to you so that you will make progress and advance in your Christian life." Paul told Timothy to *take pains with these things; be absorbed in them, so that your progress will be evident to all* (1 Timothy 4:15). We can grow and mature in our Christian life.

***Helpfulness and happiness go together.**$

One of the ways people grow and mature in their Christian life is by mentoring others. Older, more mature Christians can be a tremendous blessing to younger, inexperienced Christians. Paul mentored Timothy. If we really want to enjoy life, we need to find a young Christian and be an encouragement to them.

Inspirational

But if I am to live on in the flesh, this will mean fruitful labor (Philippians 1:22). Paul was saying, "I am convinced that my ministry to you is needful." His ministry was not only needful, but he also believed it would be **joyful**: *I will remain and continue with you all for your progress and joy in the faith* (Philippians 1:25).

Do we bring joy into other people's lives? When people see us coming, are they glad or sad? Are we a misery or a ministry? Paul said he was "convinced that my ministry to you will be joyful and will bring happiness to your life."

Helpfulness and happiness go together. The more helpful we are to other people, the happier we personally are going to be. In fact, happiness is kind of like a perfume. We cannot splash it on ourselves without splashing some on others. If someone wants to be miserable, they will live for themselves. If someone wants to be joyful, they will live for others.

THE PARADIGMS OF A PRISONER

Booker T. Washington, an incredible scientist, said, "In meeting men in many places, I have found that the happiest people are those who do the most for others, and the most miserable are those who do the least." It is so true that when we get interested in other people and have a ministry in their lives, it brings personal joy. Our lives should be a joy to other people; and in so doing, it will be a joy to us.

Invaluable

Paul felt it was needful for the church at Philippi if he remained with them as he would help to further their progress and joy in the faith. He also said that *this will mean fruitful labor for me* (Philippians 1:22). Paul wanted to have some fruit in their lives.

The Christian life is like a fruit tree. *The righteous man will flourish like the palm tree, he will grow like a cedar in Lebanon. Planted in the house of the Lord, they will flourish in the courts of our God. They will still yield fruit in old age; they shall be full of sap and very green* (Psalm 92.12-14). What a statement!

Unfortunately, some fruit trees stop bearing fruit and become unproductive. However, that does should not be true of the Christian life. According to Psalm 92:14, people can still bear fruit in old age.

Paul taught us his philosophy: *For to me, to live is Christ*, and his purpose: "I am convinced that I am going to stay here for a while longer." Christians are immortal until God is through with them. If God has a job for us to do, we will stay here until God does that job in and through our lives.

WE NEED A POSITIVENESS FOR PROBLEMS.

We have now come to Paul's quandary in life. He has already summed up the great exchange that *to die is gain* (Philippians 1:21). He has already said that he is convinced that God wants him to live a little bit longer, but then he wrote: *What I shall choose I wot not. For I am in a strait betwixt two* (Philippians 1:22-23 KJV). *For I am in a strait betwixt two* describes a traveler who is going through a narrow passage with rock walls on each side. It is so narrow that he can hardly turn from side to side.

Pictures of the ancient city of Petra reveal a narrow passageway that people have to go through to get into Petra. It is so narrow that they can hardly turn from side to side.

A Delightful Dilemma

Paul was saying, "I am hemmed in. I have a delightful dilemma. Either I will stay here; and if I do, I will have a ministry in your life; or I will die, and that will be gain. I don't know whether it is better to live or whether it is better to die."

For most of us, that is not a dilemma. Faced with the decision of living or dying, we would choose life every time. Yet Paul wrote, "I am in a quandary. I am hemmed in. I am pulled in two directions. I have a desire to depart and be with Christ which is far better, but I also a desire to stay here and minister to you."

Paul really believed what he said about death, but do we? Has it really gripped our hearts as believers? Do we believe that death for the believer is to depart and be with Christ and it is far better? As a born-again believer, Paul could say it as can we because for the believer, death means escape from earth's sorrows and problems to be with Christ.

The word "depart" in the phrase, *having the desire to depart* (Philippians 1:23), is a very picturesque word in the Greek language. It is sometimes used as a military term and pictures a battle-worn soldier who is getting ready to pull up the stakes of his tent and move out. For Paul, it was his desire to pull up the stakes of his old earthly tent and depart for heaven.

Paul describes the life of a believer as being like a tent: *For we know that if the earthly tent which is our house is torn down, we have a building from God, a house not made with hands, eternal in the heavens* (2 Corinthians 5:1). For the believer, death is like a soldier, striking stakes and moving on.

The word "depart" was also used as a nautical term. It is a picture of a sailor who had sailed through stormy seas and would soon land on shore and be home again. Paul was saying, "I have a desire to depart like a weary sailor." *The time of my departure has come* (2 Timothy 4:6) meaning his death was the departure. He was saying, "I'm getting ready to break loose from the shores of time and earth and embark on the great sea of eternity and land on the glorious shores of heaven." As believers, the heavenly shores are ahead of us as we depart this stormy life.

For those going through earthly sorrows, death will be a release.

For those going through earthly sorrows, death will be a release. There are people who never have a wakeful moment without pain, and it is even difficult for them to sleep at night due to their pain-wracked body. One day, death will mean release from earth's pains.

Consider the tearful goodbyes to loved ones, watching them slip into eternity. They leave an empty chair at the table and a void in our hearts. To depart and be with Christ means that one day, there will be no more separations.

To depart and be with Christ means that the day will come when we will battle sin no longer. Verse 3 of the hymn, "There Is a Fountain Filled with Blood," says, "Till all the ransomed church of God are saved to sin no more." The hymn was written by William Cowper in 1771 or 1772, based on Zechariah 13:1. Cowper suffered from depression and found hope in the redemption of Christ and faith in the cleansing power of the blood of Christ and his anticipation of a heavenly song. We rejoice for the time will come when we will never again have to repent of sin or suffer with a broken heart because of our failures. What a relief it will be when we cross to the heavenly side.

If we really believe God's Word, we should not dread death. Death is like a bird in a shell. The bird begins to struggle and push and then after a while, the shell cracks open and the bird emerges. The bird does not mourn its departure from the shell that had restricted it.

The soldier battling the enemy on the front lines faces danger every moment. His meals have been poor and pathetic. Then the word comes: "Get ready! You are leaving for a few days of R&R." The soldier does not mourn leaving the fox hole and the less-than-tasty food for rest and peace and joy.

Having the desire to depart and be with Christ (Philippians 1:23) means release from earth's problems.

A Divine Departure

Death for the believer means the realization of Christ's presence. There is a sense, of course, in which we are with Christ right now. Jesus said that *where two or three have gathered together in My name, I am there in their midst* (Matthew 18:20) which means that Jesus is with us now.

However, there is a sense that to depart is to be with Christ in an even fuller way. In life, Jesus is with us; in death, we are with Christ. We truly cannot imagine how glorious it will be to step into the very presence of Jesus Christ.

Don Wyrtzen wrote "Finally Home" with a chorus that states: "Just think of stepping on shore and finding it heaven, of touching a hand and finding it God's, of breathing new air and finding it celestial, of waking up in glory and finding it home." These are the delights of death for the believer. It is no wonder Paul said, "I can't figure out which I would rather do, stay here or go there."

However, we cannot have Paul's philosophy of death unless we also have Paul's philosophy of life. A good exercise would be to take a piece of paper and write: "For me, to live is _____," and then fill in the blank. Some may say, "For me, to live is money" or "For me, to live is popularity" or "For me, to live is football" or "For me, to live is my boyfriend or girlfriend" or "For me, to live is my business" or "For me, to live is my family."

Death for the believer means the realization of Christ's presence.

We must recognize that two phrases in Philippians 1:21 cannot be changed: *to live*...and...*to die*. Paul said, *For me, to live is Christ*. If any word is put in the blank except *Christ*, then the words, *to die is gain*, must be changed to "to die is loss" because all is loss except Christ.

Hopefully, we can all truthfully write, "For me, to live is Christ," and then we can also write, "And to die is gain."

7

LIVING LIKE WE ARE DYING

Tim McGraw recorded the song, "Live Like You Were Dying"; and it won several awards, including Single of the Year and Song of the Year at the 2004 Country Music Association Awards and the 2004 Academy of Country Music Awards and the 2004 Grammy Award for Best Country Song. This song was really what the Apostle Paul was talking about when he said *whether by life or by death* (Philippians 1:20) and *for to me, to live is Christ and to die is gain* (Philippians 1:21). To live and to die: the two ultimate outcomes.

In Philippians 1, the Apostle Paul gave us three incredible pictures of life. *In view of your participation in the gospel from the first day until now* (v.5), we note that Paul was thankful for the fellowship in the gospel. The picture is of the Christian life as being a son sharing the fellowship of the gospel. We are sons and daughters in Christ and are to share with one another the fellowship of the gospel.

In the second picture, Paul wrote about the furtherance of the gospel: *Now I want you to know, brethren, that my circumstances have turned out for the greater progress of the gospel* (v.12). This picture is of a Christian being a servant, seeking the furtherance of the gospel. We are sons sharing the fellowship of the gospel and servants seeking the furtherance of the gospel.

The Christian life is not a playground but a battleground.

In the third picture, Paul taught that we are to strive together for the faith of the gospel. *Only conduct yourselves in a manner worthy of the gospel of Christ, so that whether I come and see you or remain absent, I will hear of you that you are standing firm in one spirit, with one mind striving together for the faith of the gospel* (Philippians 1:27). This picture is that Christians are like soldiers striving for the faith of the gospel. If we listen carefully to these verses, we will hear the marching of troops and the sound of gunfire. Paul pictured the Christian life as that of a soldier's.

Of course, we know that soldiers must live like they are dying because they are always in places of danger. They know their life is up for grabs and death may be imminent at any moment.

We need to understand that the Christian life is not a playground but a battleground. It is not a frolic but a fight; it is not a stroll but a struggle. As believers, we should live every day like we are dying, keeping in mind that as believers, we are soldiers of the cross and are going into battle for Jesus Christ.

OUR CONDUCT MUST BE CONSISTENT.

If we are going to live like we are dying, the first thing we notice is that our conduct and daily life must be consistent.

The New Living Translation of Philippians 1:27 says that *above all, you must live as citizens of heaven, conducting yourselves in a manner worthy of the Good News about Christ.* The city of Philippi was a Roman colony and was governed by Roman law. The Philippians were to emulate the patterns and the lifestyles of Rome. When Paul said, *You must live as citizens of heaven*, they would immediately have understood him. Although they were citizens of the Roman Empire, they knew they must let their heavenly citizenship be demonstrated by their consistent life as born-again believers.

Paul wrote about two qualities of our conduct as believers. First, our conduct needs to be befitting of the gospel by living *as citizens of heaven, conducting* [ourselves] *in a manner worthy of the Good News about Christ*. Our daily life should be lived by the standards of the gospel.

Heavenly standards should be the standards whereby we govern our conduct.

When we visit a foreign country, we are still citizens of America and are bound by the standards and laws of our homeland. The same is true regarding believers. We belong to heaven; therefore, heavenly standards should be the standards whereby we govern our conduct.

Our culture has its own standards—its own rules regarding right and wrong. For instance, one standard is that if it feels right, we should do it. In that manner, we become our own standard of what is right and wrong regarding our behavior and conduct. However, if we name the name of Jesus and are a citizen of heaven, we have a different set of standards. We do not live by the standards of this world but by the standards of heaven. Paul said our conduct must be consistent and befitting of the gospel of the Lord Jesus Christ.

Additionally, we should live in a manner that is becoming of the gospel. The King James Version of Philippians 1:27 says to *let [our] conversation be as it becometh the gospel of Christ.* Any woman who has been told, "That dress becomes you," knows she has been given a compliment. The person who gave the compliment was saying, "You are lovely, and your dress just accentuates your loveliness."

As born-again believers in Christ, we are called to live in such a way that we make the gospel beautiful to others. The gospel is beautiful because it tells how God so loved the world that He sent His only Son who came into the world and died on a cross for our sins, was buried, and three days later rose again from the dead. He is alive forevermore to change the lives of mankind.

If we are going to live like we are dying, then we must live in such a way that our life will attract people to the gospel of Christ. We must strive to be the greatest product the world has ever known because if people just knew how wonderful Jesus is, they would beg to come to know Him. The best advertisement any church can have is for believers to live for Jesus on the job, in their social circles, and in their neighborhoods and communities. By doing so, those who watch their lives will want to come to their respective churches to find out what makes believers live the way they do.

OUR COURAGE MUST BE EVIDENT.

Only conduct yourselves in a manner worthy of the gospel of Christ, so that whether I come and see you or remain absent, I will hear of you that you are standing firm in one spirit, with one mind striving together for the faith of the gospel (Philippians 1:27). Paul reminds us that our courage must be evident by our faithfulness. *That you are standing firm in one spirit* means to be united—standing side by side.

In present days, God's people need courage. New ideas of morality regarding marriage are being pushed in our public schools, and our Christian students need courage to take a stand for Jesus Christ in order to be united in their faith in the Lord.

Additionally, Paul stated that we must *[stand] firm in one spirit*. In the spirit of Winston Churchill, we need to be resolved in our courage. When England was under attack by the Nazis during World War II, Churchill said, "We shall not flag or fail. We shall go on to the end.... We shall never surrender!" (House of Commons, June 4, 1940, following the evacuation of British and French armies from Dunkirk as the German tide swept through France). That is the kind of spirit we need today on the part of God's people.

Our courage must be evident by our faithfulness and our fearlessness.

With one mind striving together for the faith of the gospel. Using athletic terminology, not only was Paul saying that we should put up a good front and have a good defense, but he also was saying that we should have a good offense.

One of the greatest things in the world of college football is to have a good offense with a good quarterback, a good running back, and a big offensive line. The children of God are a great team for the Lord Jesus Christ. We need not always be on the defensive because there are times when we need to be on the offensive. If we are going to live like we are dying, we must be faithful to the Lord.

Our courage must be evident by our *faithfulness* and our *fearlessness*. Paul told us *in no way [be] alarmed by your opponents* (Philippians 1:28). We are not to be terrified of our enemies or of those we are fighting against. There are many Christians who live in great fear and run when they are under attack crying, "What are we going to do? We are under attack! I'm terrified!"

However, we have nothing to fear because we are members of God's victorious team!

When horses are terrified, they experience an intense level of fear and may exhibit extreme physical signs such as trembling or sweating profusely. They may also be more likely to bolt or rear up in an attempt to escape the source of their fear. However, war horses were trained to hold firm in a battle and not flinch. That is how we as God's people should be in our battles with our adversary. We must remember that if we are a child of God, we are immortal until God says otherwise. We belong to Christ and must not be terrified of our enemies when they attack our values and morals.

The story is told about a great preacher who was taking a stand against false doctrine. Someone said to him, "Don't you understand that the whole world is against you?" He responded, "I'm against the whole world." If we know we are right and are standing on biblical truth with the Lord Jesus Christ, we must take our stand and not be afraid.

The King James Version phrases Philippians 1:28 as, *And in nothing terrified by your adversaries: which is to them an evident token of perdition*. In other words, the fact that we are unafraid and stand with courage for what is right is a token or evidence that they are on the losing side and on their way to hell and need Jesus. However, not only is it evidence that they are on the losing side, but it is also a token to us of salvation: *And in nothing terrified by your adversaries: which is to them an evident token of perdition, but to you of salvation, and that of God.*

One of the ways we can know we are saved is when we are attacked by Satan. Does hell know our name? Do those in hell know who we are? We should live for Jesus with such courage that we are a conversation piece in the hot halls of hell.

We have a token or evidence of our salvation, and that of God. In the New Testament era in Rome, gladiator games were held at the Coliseum. When the fight was over, the gladiator would look up to the emperor's box, and the emperor would give either a thumbs up or a thumbs down. We must be courageous for Christ and look to heaven. If we stand for the Lord Jesus, He will give us a thumbs up. We need to live like we are dying.

OUR CHRISTLIKENESS MUST BE TRIUMPHANT.

For to you it has been granted for Christ's sake, not only to believe in Him, but also to suffer for His sake, experiencing the same conflict which you saw in me, and now hear to be in me (Philippians 1:29-30). Many Christians wish these words were not in the Bible and do not want to hear them in relation to the Christian life because they are spoiled and pampered and prefer to hear about prosperity, health, and wealth instead. If the air conditioning in the church goes out, they feel as though they are really suffering for Jesus; but Paul was talking about Christlikeness—suffering for the sake of Christ.

Suffering is a part of the salvation package.

Paul spoke in unusual terms of the gift of suffering. Why are we given the gift of suffering? Paul said it was given to us not only to believe in Him but also to suffer for Him—that suffering is a part of the salvation package because the Lord told him on the Damascus Road that I will show him how much he must suffer for My name's sake (Acts 9:16). Suffering is a tool God uses to help us become what He has saved us to become. Suffering is a means of learning lessons we could learn in no other way.

It has been said that every sorrow comes with a message from the heart of God. Suffering is a love gift from the Lord. God honors us by the amount of suffering He allows us to experience in our life. A general puts his strongest and best soldiers in the hottest part of the battle. If we are suffering, it is a compliment.

In the Bible, the "gift of suffering" and the "glory of suffering" are tied together. Jesus suffered, but He also was glorified. He said of Himself, *Was it not necessary for the Christ to suffer these things and to enter into His glory?* (Luke 24:26). Suffering is the road to glory. Our Christlikeness becomes triumphant when we learn to suffer like Jesus did.

There are far too many Christians in the nosebleed section of life.

For I consider that the sufferings of this present time are not worthy to be compared with the glory that is to be revealed to us (Romans 8:18.) *For momentary, light affliction is producing for us an eternal weight of glory far beyond all comparison* (2 Corinthians 4:17). God has some glory that He wants to put in our life. We must live like we are dying so that our Christlikeness will be triumphant.

Philippians 1 concludes with the words, *experiencing the same conflict which you saw in me, and now hear to be in me* (v.30). The word *conflict* in this context is the same word that was used of Jesus in the Garden of Gethsemane. Jesus went through the agony; but when the agony of Gethsemane was over, He had the victory of the cross.

Just as Jesus and Paul and the believers throughout the centuries have done, it is time for present-day Christians to get "in the game," again using athletic terminology. We live in an era when the grandstands are filled with 80,000-100,000 fans watching their favorite football team play. Imagine a man sitting in the "nosebleed section" telling to his buddies, "If I were the coach, I'd manage this team differently. Look at our quarterback. He can hardly play. Why do they run the plays they run?"

This man will "talk the talk" but cannot "walk the walk." He is content to criticize or cheer throughout the game. If his favorite team wins, he will no doubt exclaim, "We showed 'em! We have a mighty winning team!" However, he nothing to help the team win; he made no blocks or runs the entire game.

Unfortunately, there are far too many Christians in the nosebleed section of life. They love to cheer when things go well and criticize when they go wrong. It is time for the Christians of this generation to get on the playing field of life and fight the good fight of faith. Conflict and suffering will be part of the story; but in the end, we will be triumphant for *we are more than conquerors through him that loved us* (Romans 8:37). We must live like we are dying.

THE PATTERNS OF THE CHRISTIAN LIFE
(PHILIPPIANS 2:1-30)

8

OTHERS

William Booth, an English Methodist preacher who, along with his wife, Catherine, founded the Salvation Army and became its first General. He led in spreading the gospel over much of the world as he organized street meetings and evangelistic services. With the passing of the years, his eyesight failed him, and one year he was in such bad health that he was unable to attend the Salvation Army Convention in London, England. Someone had suggested that he send a telegram to be read at the opening of the convention, and General Booth agreed to do so.

When the thousands of delegates met, the moderator announced that General Booth would not be able to be present because of failing health and eyesight. Gloom and pessimism swept across the floor of the convention. However, a little light dispelled some of the darkness when the moderator announced that General Booth had sent a message to be read at the opening of the first session. He opened the message and began to read.

Dear Delegates of the Salvation Army Convention:

OTHERS!

Signed, General Booth

Therefore if there is any encouragement in Christ, if there is any consolation of love, if there is any fellowship of the Spirit, if any affection and compassion, make my joy complete by being of the same mind, maintaining the same love, united in spirit, intent on one purpose. Do nothing from selfishness or empty conceit, but with humility of mind regard one another as more important than yourselves; do not merely look out for your own personal interests, but also for the interests of others (Philippians 2:1-4).

A wise man once said, "There is no life so empty as a self-centered life and no life so centered as a self-emptied life." When we are preoccupied with ourselves, we are miserable. When we let Jesus Christ love others through us, we have the joy that Christian fellowship is intended to give to us all.

The church at Philippi was certainly a source of great joy and satisfaction to its founder, the Apostle Paul. There had been a series of conversions which formed the nucleus of the church. In Paul's letter to the church, we find love, appreciation, and gratitude for those wonderful Philippian believers.

Nevertheless, the church at Philippi was not perfect. When we read about the New Testament churches, we get the idea that they were perfect with no flaws whatsoever. However, there are no perfect churches. A church sign once read, "No Perfect People Welcome Here."

The church is not a trophy case for the exhibition of perfect saints but a school for the education of imperfect believers. We are all growing in the Lord and seeking to be what God wants us to be. A church, even a "good" church, is going to have difficulties and problems within. Satan is not going to disturb a sleeping church nor resurrect a dying church. Consequently, if there are problems in the midst of a church, it is probably an indication that Satan is at work because something good is going on in that church.

The church is not a trophy case for the exhibition of perfect saints but a school for the education of imperfect believers.

In Philippians 4, we learn there is a problem in the church at Philippi. Perhaps it is not a major problem at that particular point, but Paul was aware that one was brewing because there was a slight flaw in the harmony of the church. In the opening verses of Philippians 2, Paul tenderly and tactfully began to move towards working out the problem. He issued a call to unity as the church was to be a group of people who share things in common, possess unity and harmony, and have togetherness of spirit.

Paul knew we must all come to the point where we put "others" ahead of ourselves. Paul began the chapter with the word "if"—not to raise doubt but to express certainty. In the opening statements where "if" is used four times, he was basically giving us the four reasons why and the four incentives to spiritual togetherness on the part of the members of a fellowship.

The Christian life is not merely believing a set of doctrines or going by a set of rules. Christianity is a relationship with a person, the Lord Jesus Christ. Because of that relationship with Jesus and because we are united in the Lord, we are related to one another. Jesus prayed that His disciples *may all be one* (John 17:21). The first incentive is our **relationship to the Lord.**

Paul then spoke of the comfort or incentive of **love:** *if there is any consolation of love* (Philippians 2:1). The love which Jesus Christ has for us is an incentive for us to love one another. When Jesus comes into our heart, He creates a love in us for others.

He said, *A new commandment I give to you, that you love one another, even as I have loved you, that you also love one another* (John 13:34).

The third incentive Paul spoke of was the **fellowship of the Holy Spirit**. When Christ comes into our hearts, He comes in the person of the Holy Spirit. Every born-again believer is indwelt by the Holy Spirit. It is the Holy Spirit's fellowship, the communion of the Holy Spirit, that brings us together. Christ and the Holy Spirit put a desire in our hearts to be compassionate, tender, loving, and forgiving to one another.

The church was to be a group of people who share things in common, possess unity and harmony, and have togetherness of spirit.

If there is encouragement in Christ, consolation of love, fellowship of the Spirit, and affection and compassion, Paul said it would make his *joy complete* (Philippians 2:2). "Joy" is a recurring word throughout the Book of Philippians. Paul's cup of joy was already full, but he knew there was room for a few more drops. "If you will be one in the Lord, if you will be together, if you will have unity in the Lord, then you will fill my cup of joy to the brim and overflowing."

When there are problems of unity, it affects our joy in the Lord; but when there is unity and togetherness on the part of God's people, it is a source of great joy. These are days when God's people need to be together in our fellowship like never before.

On the basis of the spiritual realities and incentives, Paul gives us the ingredients of what will keep a church together and *make [his] joy complete*.

WE SHOULD ENCOURAGE HARMONY IN THE CHURCH.

Ingredient number one is harmony. *Make my joy complete by being of the same mind, maintaining the same love, united in spirit, intent on one purpose* (Philippians 2:2). To be *of the same mind* means to think the same thing. It is beautiful when God's people are in harmony together.

Unity does not necessarily mean uniformity.

Psalm 133, the fourth shortest chapter in the Bible, begins by saying, *Behold, how good and how pleasant it is for brothers to dwell together in unity!* When there is love between the saints, the Lord's presence will be real among them.

Unity does not necessarily mean uniformity or that we all think alike or that we are all in lockstep. There is a difference between unity and uniformity. Take two tomcats, tie them together, and throw them over a clothesline. There may be uniformity, but there definitely is NO unity.

The world would desire to make uniformists of all of us—to make us all just alike. To dress alike. If there is any doubt, go to a high school campus and see how the students are dressed. If there is further question, go to an office and see how employees clothe themselves. The world wants us all to dress alike and talk alike.

However, God is a god of great variety. Look at the incredible number of different animals in a zoo. Individuals are all originals; but when Christ comes into our life, there is the making of a great harmony among the people of the Lord.

When Paul said to be *of the same mind* or likeminded, he did not mean that we all have to think the same or agree on every point. It does mean though that we must learn to disagree in a spirit of love—learn to celebrate our differences and take those differences and put them together for the greater good of the body of Christ.

After Paul tells us to be *of the same mind* (Philippians 2:2), he uses three terms: *maintaining the same love, united in spirit,* and *intent on one purpose.* The key is loving the Lord Jesus Christ. When we love Jesus and we love Jesus together, we have the makings of a great harmony in the fellowship of the people.

Paul then said, *intent on one purpose.* Our souls are united together in spirit. When we think of an orchestra, there are many different kinds of instruments including flutes, violins, trumpets, trombones, and percussion. The reason the orchestra sounds so good when it plays is because the members are all in tune with one another. The same thing is true in the fellowship of a church. We must be *of one mind* (KJV)—focused on the same purpose.

Many churches do not have harmony because they do not know what a church is supposed to be or what a church is supposed to do. The reason the New Testament church had such tremendous harmony is because they knew exactly what they were to be and exactly what they were to do.

Many churches seem to have no clue what they are supposed to be doing. They do not know their purpose and think they are a glorified social club or country club.

The church was established to give every person within the sphere of the church's influence an opportunity to know Jesus Christ as their Lord and Savior. If we do not know our purpose or how to accomplish it, we will not be in harmony. However, if we study Scripture and find that our purpose is to win people to faith in the Lord Jesus Christ and if we unite together for that purpose, there will be tremendous harmony in the fellowship.

WE SHOULD EMBRACE HUMILITY IN THE CHURCH.

The second ingredient of spiritual togetherness is humility. *Do nothing from selfishness or empty conceit, but with humility of mind regard one another as more important than yourselves* (Philippians 2:3).

Verse 3 contains both a negative statement and a positive statement. *Let nothing be done through strife or vainglory* (KJV) is the negative statement. In the fellowship of a church, nothing should be done that is motivated by strife or vainglory (excessive pride) if the body wants to stay together.

Every age group within the church is important.

D. L. Moody stated that "strife is pulling another down, and vainglory is putting one's self up." The original word for strife was used to describe someone seeking political office, one who was willing to do whatever necessary in order to win that office. It is the idea that people are trying to climb the ladder of success and care not how many people they step on or push aside. They are totally interested in their own personal self-advancement and ambition.

It also gives the idea of a "party spirit"; and if not watchful, a church can develop that spirit. Sometimes churches focus on special groups; however, we must be careful not to get into that mindset because every age group within the church is important. We are called to be the "family of God." The older people in the church are just as vital as the middle-agers, the young adults, and the teenagers and children. Each age group has need of the other.

Cliques often form in a church and become small social clubs. Although there is nothing wrong with having close friends, we do not exist just for our own little group. When we develop the attitude of how every decision will affect our own particular group, we move into the realm of strife—into the area of personal ambition and personal advancement.

Paul did not want the Philippian church to do anything with an attitude of "what will a particular decision do for us or to us personally." Paul admonished them not to do anything based on selfishness and personal conceit for that would be prideful and they would end up being full of themselves.

Is what we do in our own church for the honor and glory of the Lord or for personal attention? Will those who are members of the choir but are never called on to sing a solo continue to sing in the choir? Will those who are not elected as a deacon continue to witness for Jesus on their job? Will those who are not appointed to one of the key committees of the church still be faithful to Christ? Will we continue to pray and read our Bible? It is not about us; it is about Jesus. *Do nothing from selfishness or empty conceit.*

We are not saved by any greatness or goodness on our part.

Paul then turned to the positive: *but with humility of mind regard one another as more important than yourselves* or as expressed in the King James Version: *but in lowliness of mind let each esteem others better than themselves.* Lowliness of mind is the concept of humility.

Humble people are not just those who think of themselves as less important than others but those who do not think about themselves at all. There is far too much pride among the people of God. God desires that we be humble before Him—lowly in our attitude. Humility is a very elusive virtue. In fact, it is so elusive that the moment we think we have it, we lose it. The joke goes something like: Did you hear about the guy who won the humility button at church? They took it away from him because he wore it.

The Christian life begins with humility—with humbling ourselves as a little child and coming to Christ at the foot of the cross saying, "God, I'm a poor, hell-bound sinner. I don't deserve to be saved." We are not saved by any greatness or goodness on our part. After we have given our lives to Christ, we must stay at the foot of the cross and keep the attitude that "I'm the slave; He's the Master. I'm the child; He's the Father."

We must always keep a spirit of humility before the Lord. If we do, it will solve a lot of problems in our relationships with other. Too often we get the idea that "I have to be first"; but humility says that "I am willing to be second or even last." May God help us to stay humble before the Lord. There are no big shots or little shots in the family of God. We are all God's people—sinners who have been saved by a wonderful Savior.

WE SHOULD EXEMPLIFY HELPFULNESS IN THE CHURCH.

Paul gives us the third ingredient of spiritual togetherness which is helpfulness. *Do not merely look out for your own personal interests, but also for the interests of others* (Philippians 2:4). *For they all seek after their own interests, not those of Christ Jesus* (Philippians 2:21), In other words, their attitude is that of looking out for number one—themselves.

If we want spiritual togetherness in our fellowship, there must be willingness not to seek after our own things or put ourselves as number one. Helpfulness is an attitude of considering others. The world would have us believe that the way to be happy is to only take care of ourselves—that the way to spell joy is to put ourselves first, others second, and the Lord not at all. That is why there are so many people with dysfunctional lives in our world.

The same is true in marriage. Many couples have trouble in their marriages because they go into the relationship with the attitude of "what will my spouse be able to do for me?" If we go into a marriage with that kind of attitude, we are headed for problems. We should marry with the attitude of "it is not what my spouse can do for me but what I can do for my spouse" that is important. It is an unselfish spirit that will cause a marriage to work.

When we join a church, our attitude should not be, "What is this church going to do for me?" but "What can I do for Jesus through the fellowship of this church?" People often say, "I didn't get a thing out of the service today." The correct questions to ask would be: "What did they put into the service today? Who did they encourage today? Who did they bless today? Did they pray today?"

It is an unselfish spirit that will cause a marriage to work.

Do not merely look out for your own personal interests, but also for the interests of others. Some will invariably say, "Don't do it! You'll get walked on that way. Stand up for yourself!"

Consider Abraham and Lot. They came to a point where they had to go their separate ways. God was blessing them so much they needed to expand their territory. Abraham said to Lot, *Please let there be no strife between you and me, nor between my herdsmen and your herdsmen, for we are brothers. Is not the whole land before you? Please separate from me; if to the left, then I will go to the right; or if to the right, then I will go to the left* (Genesis 13:8-9). Lot made a selfish choice and eventually lost his family and his fortune and almost his faith. On the other hand, Abraham was willing to take second place, and God said to Him, *Now lift up your eyes and look from the place where you are, northward and southward and eastward and westward; for all the land which you see, I will give it to you and to your descendants forever* (Genesis 13:14-15).

When we are willing to put others first and ourselves last, we are on the path to joy. In fact, that is how to spell joy in the Book of Philippians. Chapter 1 is about Jesus – put Jesus first. Chapter 2 is about others – put others second. Chapter 3 is about us individually – put "yourself" last. J-O-Y. No wonder Paul could write, *make my joy complete* (Philippians 2:2). Paul lived with fullness of joy and wanted others to be filled also!

9

THE GOD-MAN

Millions of people are asking the question, "Who is Jesus Christ?" A lot of them do not find Him because they are looking in the wrong places. Some years ago, Bryant Gumbel interviewed Larry King on national television; and at the close of the interview, Gumbel asked King a question—a very pertinent question: "Larry, if you could meet God and ask Him one question, what would it be?" King replied, "I would ask Him if He has a Son." Great question!

The world will never be able to answer the sin question until it answers the Son question.

When you see documentaries on television about Jesus, they are couched with words such as, "Jesus—Who Was He?" That is the wrong question. The proper question would be, "Jesus—Who

Is He?" The world does not understand the Lord Jesus Christ; consequently, the world will never be able to answer the sin question until it answers the Son question: Who is Jesus?

> *Have this attitude in yourselves which was also in Christ Jesus, who, although He existed in the form of God, did not regard equality with God a thing to be grasped, but emptied Himself, taking the form of a bond-servant, and being made in the likeness of men. Being found in appearance as a man, He humbled Himself by becoming obedient to the point of death, even death on a cross. For this reason also, God highly exalted Him, and bestowed on Him the name which is above every name, so that at the name of Jesus every knee will bow, of those who are in heaven and on earth and under the earth, and that every tongue will confess that Jesus Christ is Lord, to the glory of God the Father* (Philippians 2:5-11).

It is estimated that approximately 100 billion people have lived in recorded history on planet earth. Out of those billions, only a handful have risen to such prominence that they could have affected human history. However, there is one name that stands out above all of the others, and that is the name of Jesus Christ. Jesus is genuinely unique. No other person has ever attracted such a combination of attention, devotion, criticism, adoration, and opposition as Jesus Christ. He is the focal point of all theological discussions. Theologians, philosophers, and historians have studied this one solitary life—the life of our Lord and Savior Jesus Christ, Jesus of Nazareth who lived approximately 2,000 years ago in a small country called Israel. His birth date divides the timeline into B.C. and A.D.—"Before Christ" and "Anno Domini" or "the year of our Lord."

As far as we know, Jesus never wrote a book; yet more books have been written about Him than any person who has ever lived. As far as we know, He never painted a picture, did any sculpting, wrote a poem, or composed music; yet Jesus of Nazareth has been the inspiration for artists, sculptors, poets, and musicians. The world is full of music about Jesus, the Christ, the Son of God. As far as we know, Jesus Christ never raised an army; yet millions have died for Him and for His cause. He traveled only a few miles from His birthplace throughout His ministry; however, His ministry reaches around the world. He never spoke to more than a few thousand people at one time, but for 24 hours—every day that the clock goes around—at any moment of that 24 hours, there are millions of people studying what He said. Whenever we check the time, there will be millions of people studying His Word.

To explain Jesus Christ is impossible, to ignore Him is disastrous, to refuse Him is fatal.

His ministry lasted only three brief years; yet His message is still going around the world by radio, television, and the Internet. He had no formal education; yet His life has inspired the founding of more colleges, seminaries, and universities than any other. To explain Jesus Christ is impossible, to ignore Him is disastrous, to refuse Him is fatal. Words are too limited to describe Him, the human mind is too finite to comprehend Him, and people's hearts are too small to contain all the love that the Lord Jesus has for every person who has ever been born in the entire world.

JESUS IS THE SUPERNATURAL SON OF GOD.

Jesus, *who, although He existed in the form of God, did not regard equality with God a thing to be grasped* (Philippians 2:6), is the supernatural Son of God. He was preexisting in the form of God—pure Spirit—*but emptied Himself, taking the form of a bond-servant, and being made in the likeness of men* (Philippians 2:7). The Infinite became an infant through a virgin birth—a fulfillment of Isaiah 7:14: *Therefore the Lord Himself will give you a sign: Behold, a virgin will be with child and bear a son.*

Many people throughout history have found it hard to believe that Jesus was born of a virgin. The first person to doubt was Mary herself, saying to the angel, *How can this be, since I am a virgin?* (Luke 1:34). And the angel answered Mary, *Nothing will be impossible with God* (Luke 1:37).

When a person does not believe in the virgin birth, it indicates a character problem. They have a problem with the character of the Word of God. They have a problem with the character of Mary because if Jesus was not born of a virgin, Mary was unmarried and therefore a harlot. They have a problem with the character of Jesus because if Jesus was not born of a virgin, He was born out of wedlock and was a son of Adam and *in Adam all die* (1 Corinthians 15:22). Consequently, He would not have been the sinless Son of God. They also have a problem with their own character for without the virgin birth, we have no hope of salvation.

Envision Jesus in the temple at the age of 12. The teachers, wise men, and sages question him saying, "How old are you, son?" He might have smiled and said, "Well, on my mother's side, I am 12 years old; but on my father's side, I'm older than my mother and as old as my father." He was the supernatural Son of God *who, although He existed in the form of God, did not regard equality with God a thing to be grasped, but emptied Himself, taking the form of a bond-servant, and being made in the likeness of men* (Philippians 2:6-7).

JESUS IS THE SINLESS SON OF GOD.

Being found in appearance as a man, He humbled Himself by becoming obedient (Philippians 2:8). Concerning His Father, He said, *I always do the things that are pleasing to Him* (John 8:29).

Not one time did Jesus ever transgress the Father's will. God the Father said of Him, *This is my beloved Son, with whom I am well pleased* (Matthew 3:17, 17:5; 2 Peter 1:17).

They were criticizing and critiquing Jesus Christ; and He said to them, *Which one of you convicts Me of sin?* (John 8:46). He was the sinless Son of God. Satan unleashed all of the artillery of hell against Jesus, but Satan never once persuaded Jesus to sin. Satan has no trophies that he can hang on his wall indicating Jesus Christ ever sinned. Jesus said, *I will not speak much more with you, for the ruler of the world is coming, and he has nothing in Me* (John 14:30). There was no temptation that Satan could offer Jesus that He would succumb to because He is the sinless Son of God.

JESUS IS THE SOVEREIGN SON OF GOD.

Jesus is God in the flesh *who, although He existed in the form of God, did not regard equality with God a thing to be grasped* (Philippians 2:6).

The Muslims, Jews, Mormons, and Jehovah's Witnesses do not believe that Jesus is the Son of God nor God the Son. Some may ask, "By whose authority is He God the Son?" By God's authority for Jehovah spoke and said: *But of the Son He says, "Your throne, O God, is forever and ever"* (Hebrews 1:8). What does God call His Son? God.

The Pharisees, the Jewish rulers, were bantering with Jesus because Jesus had said *our father Abraham rejoiced to see My day, and he saw it and was glad* (John 8:56). They said, "Wait a minute—Abraham? He's been dead for centuries. You're not even 50 years old. How can you say, *Abraham rejoiced to see My day*?" However, they had already been boasting that *Abraham is our father* (John 8:39). What they were saying was, "We know all of that hocus-pocus about a virgin birth. *We were not born of fornication* (John 8:41)." Jesus then said something to them that rocked them back on their heels: *Before Abraham was born, I am* (John 8:58).

The most holy name that the Jews had for Jehovah was the name "I AM." When Moses was ready to lead the children of Israel from Egypt to the Promised Land, he said to God the Father, "I need some credentials. When I go to Pharaoh and to these others, I need to say under whose authority I'm operating. I need to tell them who sent me." And *God said to Moses, "I AM WHO I AM"; and He said, "Thus you shall say to the sons of Israel, 'I AM has sent me to you'"* (Exodus 3:14). God's name was "I AM"—not "I was," not "I will be"—just "I AM." "There never was a time when I was not. I will always be. I am the great 'I AM'"—a holy, sacred name for the self-existing Almighty God.

If you take away the deity of Jesus Christ, the whole house of Christianity collapses like a house of cards.

Then they said to Jesus, "How can you say that Abraham saw your day?" to which He replied, *Before Abraham was born, I am* (John 8:58). At that moment, they took up stones to kill Him because to them it was blasphemous because He clearly and plainly was making Himself coequal and coeternal with God the Father *who, although He existed in the form of God, did not regard equality with God a thing to be grasped* (Philippians 2:6).

Jesus was never created. He is God—the great "I AM." What makes the difference? If you take away the deity of Jesus Christ, the whole house of Christianity collapses like a house of cards. Jesus is the supernatural Son of God, born of a virgin. Being the supernatural Son of God, He is the sinless Son of God. And being the supernatural, sinless Son of God, He is the sovereign Son of God. He is God in human flesh. No wonder they wanted to stone Him.

This world is on the horns of a trilemma. Jesus Christ is one of three things: a lunatic, a liar, or Lord. We have to choose: deceived, deceiver, or deity. Either He is what He said He was or He knew He was not and was lying or He did not know and was a fool. Which was He? *Before Abraham was born, I am* (John 8:58).

The cross was neither incidental nor accidental.

Some may say, "That's a mystery to me." It may be a mystery, but it is a fact. *By common confession, great is the mystery of godliness: He who was revealed in the flesh, was vindicated in the Spirit, seen by angels, proclaimed among the nations, believed on in the world, taken up in glory* (1 Timothy 3:16).

JESUS IS THE SACRIFICIAL SON OF GOD.

Why God in the flesh? So that He could die for our sins. *Being found in appearance as a man, He humbled Himself by becoming obedient to the point of death, even death on a cross* (Philippians 2:8).

Why death on the cross? *For the word of the cross is foolishness to those who are perishing, but to us who are being saved it is the power of God* (1 Corinthians 1:18). The cross was neither incidental nor accidental. Christ was slain before the foundation of the world (Revelation 13:8). Before God created anything; before hanging the planets in space and flinging out the sun, moon, and stars; before scooping out the oceans and heaping up the mountains, the sacrificial death of Jesus Christ on the cross was in the heart and mind of God.

Jesus was the sacrificial Son of God because He was the sinless Son of God. Had He not been sinless, He could have died for no one's sin but His own. He would have deserved death on the cross because *the wages of sin is death* (Romans 6:23); but being the sinless Son of God, He could be our substitute.

Jesus is God in human flesh. He took *the form of a bond-servant* (Philippians 2:7); therefore, the blood that coursed through His veins was rich, red, and royal—the blood of God. Some might say, "God is Spirit, and a Spirit doesn't have blood." That was the reason for the Incarnation because *without shedding of blood there is no forgiveness* (Hebrews 9:22). God cannot forgive sin until the wages of sin are paid. The blood that was shed had to be innocent blood; it could not be blood that was inherited from Adam for *as in Adam all die* (1 Corinthians 15:22). Jesus was not a son of Adam; He was the Son of God and the Son of man at the same time.

The blood that was in Mary's body was not the blood that was in Jesus's body. The blood that flows through a mother's body is not the blood that flows through her baby's body. The mother and her baby are not interchanging blood. The mother may have one blood type and her baby a different blood type.

What determines the blood type? From where does the bloodline come? The father. In a paternity suit, it can be proven through a blood test whether a man did or did not sire the child because it is the father who determines the blood type.

Consequently, when Jesus hung His head, bled, and died on the cross, the blood that was shed was sovereign blood and, therefore, fully sacrificial blood. God was in Christ, reconciling the world unto Himself.

When Paul called the elders of the church at Ephesus together, he told them to *be on guard for yourselves and for all the flock, among which the Holy Spirit has made you overseers, to shepherd the church of God which He purchased with His own blood* (Acts 20:28). Jesus, the supernatural Son of God, is also the sinless Son of God who is the sovereign Son of God who is the sacrificial Son of God.

THE GOD-MAN

JESUS IS THE STRIVING SON OF GOD.

Death could not hold Him; He rose from the dead. *For this reason also, God highly exalted Him, and bestowed on Him the name which is above every name* (Philippians 2:9).

The grave could not hold Him because He is the Lord of both life and death. Jesus said, *No one has taken [my life] away from Me, but I lay it down on My own initiative. I have authority to lay it down, and I have authority to take it up again* (John 10:18). He survives the ages and is not in a tomb somewhere. *Therefore He is able also to save forever those who draw near to God through Him, since He always lives to make intercession for them* (Hebrews 7:25).

What makes Jesus unique? Not only His birth and His death but also His resurrection. Buddha died—and is still dead. Confucius died—and is still dead. Muhammad died—and is still dead. Jesus died also, BUT He arose and walked out of the grave! *God highly exalted Him, and bestowed on Him the name which is above every name* (Philippians 2:9).

JESUS IS THE SOON-COMING SON OF GOD.

> *For this reason also, God highly exalted Him, and bestowed on Him the name which is above every name, so that at the name of Jesus* EVERY KNEE WILL BOW, *of those who are in heaven and on earth and under the earth, and that every tongue will confess that Jesus Christ is Lord, to the glory of God the Father* (Philippians 2:9-11).

EVERY knee will bow. Satan will bow on his thorny knees and confess that Jesus Christ is Lord. The rock star Madonna will bow and confess that Jesus Christ is Lord. President Joe Biden will bow and confess that Jesus Christ is Lord. Pope Paul XI will bow and declare Jesus is the Son of God. Those who nailed Jesus to the cross will bow and confess that He is Lord. Pontius Pilate who ordered the crucifixion of Jesus will confess that Jesus is Lord. King Herod who had babies murdered will confess that Jesus is Lord.

Every person who has ever lived will meet Jesus Christ.

Every person who has ever lived will meet Jesus Christ. It is inescapable, unavoidable, and inevitable. People may not walk down an aisle and give their hearts to Jesus, but they may be rolled down an aisle at their funeral. If they do not know Jesus Christ, their soul will be in hell before the undertaker is told they are dead. On Judgment Day, they will bow before Jesus Christ and confess that He is Lord. He is the soon-coming Son of God.

After His resurrection, Jesus stood on the Mount of Olives. I have been to the Mount of Olives and wondered, "Am I standing right where Jesus stood before He ascended?" *In that day His feet will stand on the Mount of Olives, which is in front of Jerusalem on the east; and the Mount of Olives will be split in its middle from east to west by a very large valley, so that half of the mountain will move toward the north and the other half toward the south* (Zechariah 14:4).

As Jesus ascended into heaven and *as [the disciples] were gazing intently into the sky while He was going, two men in white clothing stood beside them* and *said, "Men of Galilee, why do you stand looking into the sky? This Jesus, who has been taken up from you into heaven, will come in just the same way as you have watched Him go into heaven"* (Acts 1:10-11).

Think about the feet of the Lord—those little dimpled feet that lay in the manger, those little baby feet that now bore scars. Think of those barefoot feet that walked in the shavings in Joseph's carpenter shop. Think of those sandaled feet that walked the dusty shores of Galilee. Think of those miracle feet that walked on water. Think of those nail-pierced feet on the cross. Those same feet are going to stand upon that Mount of Olives when Jesus comes again!

Christmas made Calvary possible.

Jesus is coming back—literally, visibly, and bodily to this earth. There were those who missed His first coming because they did not believe the prophecies and the Scriptures. The prophecies that were fulfilled, literally, in His first coming will be fulfilled, literally, in His Second Coming also. *At the name of Jesus* EVERY KNEE WILL BOW, *those who are in heaven and on earth and under the earth, and that every tongue will confess that Jesus Christ is Lord, to the glory of God the Father* (Philippians 2:10-11). One day the whole world will bow at his feet and declare that *Jesus Christ is Lord.*

JESUS IS THE SAVING SON OF GOD.

Being found in appearance as a man, He humbled Himself by becoming obedient to the point of death, even death on a cross (Philippians 2:8).

Why Christmas? Because of Calvary. Christmas made Calvary possible. *For the Son of Man*—God in human flesh—*has come to seek and to save that which was lost* (Luke 19:10). Jesus is the only way to be saved for *there is salvation in no one else; for there is no other name under heaven that has been given among men by which we must be saved* (Acts 4:12).

The supernatural Son of God, the sinless Son of God—God in human flesh, the sovereign Son of God—God who hung naked upon a cross, the sacrificial Son of God—God who walked out of the grave, the striving Son of God—the grave could not hold

Him, and the soon-coming Son of God became the saving Son of God—even to those on death row.

There is no sin so great that Jesus cannot forgive for His blood cleanses us from all sin.

We often think how awful it must be for a person on death row, knowing their death is so near. However, we must realize that each and every person is in the same place—on a type of death row for it is not just those on death row who are going to die. We think the one on death row must have done something HORRENDOUS to be there; however, *all have sinned and fall short of the glory of God* (Romans 3:23). It is not the fact of sin; it is the amount of sin.

The modern-day version of an ancient nursery rhyme says:

Humpty Dumpty sat on a wall,
Humpty Dumpty had a great fall.
And all the king's horses and all the king's men
Couldn't put Humpty together again.

Humpty Dumpty never met Jesus for Jesus is the One who can put us back together again. There is no sin so great that Jesus cannot forgive for His blood cleanses us from all sin.

10

THE INSIDE JOB

Being found in appearance as a man, He humbled Himself by becoming obedient to the point of death, even death on a cross (Philippians 2:8). The key word in this verse is *obedient*. Jesus obeyed, and the Bible teaches that we are to obey also. In this chapter, we will be focusing on the humility of life and living a life for others.

Disobedience is the cause of a great deal of sorrow. *For as through the one man's disobedience* [Adam] *the many were made sinners, even so through the obedience of the One* [Jesus] *the many will be made righteous* (Romans 5:19). The Bible tells us that we are to be obedient to the Lord. Philippians 2:12-13 has to do with the overall theme of how to live the Christian life, how we are to conduct ourselves as Christians, and how we can grow and mature in the Christian life. Obedience is very crucial to that entire process.

You have always obeyed, not as in my presence only, but now much more in my absence (Philippians 2:12). The church at Philippi evidently leaned heavily upon the Apostle Paul. He was away from them for a period of time and told them, "While I was there, you were obedient. Be much more obedient while I am not there."

Disobedience is the cause of a great deal of sorrow.

"Be obedient," Paul said, *much more in my absence*. He used the word, obedient, in the context of a very important subject—how we grow and develop in the Christian life. Philippians 2:12-13 explains to us how to grow in the Christian life and become everything God desires for us to be.

The Christian life is an inside job before it is an outside journey. When Christ comes into our life, He places us on the path; but the success of following the path happens first on the inside before the outside. The cliché, "fake it 'til you make it," does not work. We are to "faith it" if we are ever going to make it.

Those in our inner circle will determine the level of our success in life. While we are evaluating our enemies, we must be certain to observe our closest friends as well. In other words, we must study the inside first before working on the outside. We are going to learn the steps to growing and going in the Christian life from Philippians 2:12-13.

WE HAVE A GRAND POSSESSION.

Work out your salvation (Philippians 2:12). Our salvation is a great theme and a great possession. *How will we escape if we neglect so great a salvation?* (Hebrews 2:3).

Think of how all-encompassing salvation is. It cares for our past; we have been saved from the **penalty** of sin. It deals with our present; we are being saved from the **practice** of sin. It deals with our future; one of these days we will be saved from the very **presence** of sin.

From eternity past, love found a way.

However, we must understand that before it becomes our salvation, it is God's salvation. *Proclaim good tidings of His salvation from day to day* (Psalm 96:2).

God Planned Our Salvation

Who has saved us and called us with a holy calling, not according to our works, but according to His own purpose and grace which was granted us in Christ Jesus from all eternity (2 Timothy 1:9). God saw that we were going to be sinners and would need a Savior. From eternity past, love found a way; and God planned our salvation.

God Promised Our Salvation

In the hope of eternal life, which God, who cannot lie, promised long ages ago (Titus 1:2). All the way through the Old Testament, like a golden thread through the words and writings of the prophets, God promised this great salvation of ours. God said, "I'm going to send a Savior."

God Procured Our Salvation

God procured our salvation on the cross of Calvary by the gift of His own Son, the Lord Jesus Christ, who shed His blood for our salvation.

God Presents Our Salvation

For the wages of sin is death, but the free gift of God is eternal life in Christ Jesus our Lord (Romans 6:23). Salvation is ours because God presents it to us as a gift. When it comes to our salvation, God thought it, Jesus bought it, the Holy Spirit wrought it, the devil fought it; but praise God, we got it! It is God's salvation.

To receive Jesus Christ is to believe in Him. With the arms of faith, we reach out to take the gift of God's salvation from the nail scarred hands of the Lord Jesus Christ. Whenever it may be, at whatever age it may be, under whatever circumstances it may be, we repent of our sins; and at that moment, we receive Jesus Christ into our heart and life by faith. We are born again and can say, "It is my salvation."

WE HAVE A GODLY PROCESS.

Just as you have always obeyed, not as in my presence only, but now much more in my absence, work out your salvation (Philippians 2:12). Paul is talking about the here and now: *but now much more in my absence*. We know that salvation has to do with the great eternal future; however, the questions are: What is God doing in our life now? How is our salvation coming along now? How is the great program of working out our own salvation doing in our here and now?

The Activity of the Process

We are to work out our own salvation. The word carries the idea of continuing on to completion. It means that continuous, sustained, strenuous activity which makes our salvation everything God intends it to be in the here and now. Not only are we saved from the sins of our past and not only are we saved to go to heaven when we die, but salvation also has to do with the here and now.

Paul said to *work out your salvation*; not "work **for** your salvation." Salvation is not something we must work for or earn *for by grace you have been saved through faith; and that not of yourselves, it is the gift of God; not as a result of works, so that no one may boast. For we are His workmanship, created in Christ*

Jesus for good works, which God prepared beforehand so that we would walk in them (Ephesians 2:8-10). We cannot work something out until it has first been worked in. Salvation is God's work in us, and then we work it out.

Salvation is not something we must work for or earn.

Salvation is like a garden. We cannot work something in our garden that has not first been planted. The seed must come first, and then we work out our salvation.

Salvation is like an algebra problem. The teacher gives an algebra problem, and we begin to find a solution. However, we cannot work a problem that has not first been given to us. We work out our salvation.

Salvation is like a gold mine. Gold nuggets are found in a mine, but we must work the mine just as we do with salvation. In salvation, we learn to mine what is ours and work it out. Day after day, we are to work out our salvation.

The goal of our salvation is that we would be like Jesus. That is what predestination is all about: *For those whom He foreknew, He also predestined to become conformed to the image of His Son, so that He would be the firstborn among many brethren* (Romans 8:29).

God saved us in order that we would become like Jesus. One day in eternity, we will be like Christ; but from the moment of our salvation until the moment we are glorified, God wants us to become more and more like the Lord.

Salvation is intended to make us better. If being saved does not make us better, then what is it all about? We work it out every day.

As we work out the meaning, the ramifications, and the results of what it means to know Christ as our Savior, we should have a kinder disposition. Because we are saved, we should do kinder deeds. We should be sweeter and more loving to people. We should be living a cleaner life than we did prior to our salvation. We should have a bold witness for the Lord Jesus Christ. Every day we should be working out our own salvation.

Salvation is an inside job!

God does the work for us—salvation, then God does the work in us—sanctification, and then God does the work through us. We can cooperate with the Lord in the sanctification process—the great program of becoming like the Lord Jesus Christ.

The Attitude of the Process

Work out your salvation with fear and trembling (Philippians 2:12). What does Paul mean by that? Are we to be afraid of the Lord? Should we live our life in fear of the Lord? Paul used similar terminology in 1 Corinthians 2:3 when he talked about going to the corrupt, godless city of Corinth: *I was with you in weakness and in fear and in much trembling.* Was he afraid of Corinth? No, he was quite bold. Was he afraid that God was going to punish him if he did not minister the way he should? No, what it means is that there was an anxiety about doing what was right and not disappointing the Lord. We should live our Christian life and grow with fear and trembling, not being afraid of the Lord but with the anxious desire that we please Him in our daily life.

WE HAVE A GLORIOUS POWER.

It is God who is at work in you, both to will and to work for His good pleasure (Philippians 2:13). When we come to the Lord and begin to work out our salvation and try to become the person God intends us to be, we realize that we need power we do not have. The good news is that we do not have to live the Christian life in our own strength or try to grow as Christians in our own power for it is God who works in us.

Work out in verse 12 is different from *at work* in verse 13. In verse 12, it is the idea of working to completion to fulfill the task. In verse 13, it is where we get our word, energy, which means a manifestation of power. It is God who energizes us. *It is God who is at work in you* (Philippians 2:13). Salvation is an inside job!

When some people accept Christ as their Savior, they begin work on the outside. The truth of the matter is that God works on the inside; and when we let God work on the inside, He then changes the outside.

An unread Bible is like food uneaten.

Working just on trying to change the outside can result in a legalistic approach. Some Christians become legalists because all they do is change their outside look and habits which can cause them to be lifted up in pride. Should the outside be changed? Of course, but it is how the change comes about that is important. God begins to work in us and changes the inside of our life and gives us a different set of desires after which the outside begins to change.

An example would be when we begin to think, "I probably shouldn't be doing that anymore." God keeps working in our life; and we say, "Maybe I should stop doing that." God continues to work in our life; and we say, "My vocabulary probably needs to change." God keeps on working in our life; and we say, "Maybe my lifestyle and the way I dress should change." God uses various tools to help our salvation become everything He wants it to be.

First, **God uses the Word of God**. *For this reason we also constantly thank God that when you received the word of God which you heard from us, you accepted it not as the word of men,* *but for what it really is, the word of God, which also performs its work in you who believe* (1 Thessalonians 2:13). As we read and study the Bible, God's Word begins to work in our life.

We should appreciate the Bible because men gave their lives in order to translate it into a language we can understand. It is only within recent church history that the average person could even own a copy of God's Word. We should read our Bible every day and let it work in us because an unread Bible is like food uneaten, a love letter unread, a sword unsheathed, or a gold mine unworked.

Second, **God uses prayer in our life.** *Now to Him who is able to do far more abundantly beyond all that we ask or think, according to the power that works within us, to Him be the glory in the church and in Christ Jesus to all generations forever and ever. Amen* (Ephesians 3:20-21). It is as we pray that God works in us and in our life; He does construction in our hearts.

There is a famous story in the Book of Esther in the Old Testament about Queen Esther who needed to go before the king on behalf of the Jewish people. However, there was a custom in those days that no one could walk into the presence of the king uninvited. Unless he extended his scepter to them, it could mean death. Nevertheless, Esther went and stood at the entrance of the palace of the king. The king saw Queen Esther and extended his scepter which meant that he was in a good mood that day and she could enter.

God is a God who gives to all men liberally. He does not scold us, and there is never a time when we go to God in prayer that He is not overjoyed that we have come to Him. In fact, we can enter the very throne room of God with boldness because of the blood of Jesus. Every day of our lives, we can go into God's presence, and He will say, "Good morning! I'm so glad to see you. How long are you going to stay? I love to talk with you, and I love for you to talk to Me." God works as we pray.

Third, **God uses our sorrows, suffering, and heartaches** as tools to work in us. *For momentary, light affliction is producing* *for us an eternal weight of glory far beyond all comparison* (2 Corinthians 4:17).

I am willing to be made willing.

The Christian life is like remodeling a house. When we come to the Lord, we know we need some things done in our life. When the Lord comes on the construction scene, we say, "I think I need some new paint. Could you give me a paint job, Lord? Oh, and the roof leaks too. Could you repair my roof please, Lord?" But low and behold, when the Lord moves into our house, He starts working on our foundation. Once that is firm and sound, He begins redoing our plumbing; and the next thing we know, He is rewiring our electrical system. By now, we are beginning to get a bit uncomfortable. We just wanted God to spruce up our cottage a little; but God wants to make us into a palace and often uses suffering to accomplish His purposes.

God is working to make us more like Jesus. God who works in us both to will; that is, to make us willing, and to do; that is, to give us the power, *His good pleasure* (Philippians 2:13). God's purpose is His good pleasure.

Some people live their entire lives without purpose. They have no clue what life is all about, what they are here for, or why they are here. They get up every day. They go to their job. They drive to the same place. They eat the same food. They go through the paces of life without ever knowing the purpose and the meaning of life.

A pilot once announced to the people on his plane, "Folks, we're lost. We don't know where we are going, but don't worry. We're making good time." Do we know what we are here for? Do we know the purpose and meaning of life? If we are saved, God's purpose for our life is to be like Jesus. God will help us be willing and will give us the power to do His good will.

The Apostle Paul wrestled with this truth: *For I know that nothing good dwells in me, that is, in my flesh; for the willing is present in me, but the doing of the good is not* (Romans 7:18).

We get to the point that we desire to do God's will but then seem unable to do it. F. B. Meyer was a great Christian writer who was present at the Keswick Conference in England. He was wrestling and struggling with God's will for his life when he finally began to pray, "Dear God, I am willing to be made willing."

When we get to the point in our life that we want to grow as a Christian, be what God wants us to be, and are willing to pray, "Lord, I am willing to be made willing," then God will give us the power to be what He wants us to be.

We have a grand possession, a godly process, and a glorious power. We have all we need to make our present life priceless, purposeful, and powerful.

11

SHINING LIKE STARS IN THE UNIVERSE

The Bible abounds with figures of speech about the Christian life and provides us with lovely images describing what it encompasses.

In Philippians 2:15, the Christian life is pictured as being a child in God's family: *blameless and innocent, children of God above reproach in the midst of a crooked and perverse generation.* When we are born again, we become a member of the family of God.

In Philippians 2:17, the Christian life is compared to a sacrifice on the altar: *But even if I am being poured out as a drink offering upon the sacrifice and service of your faith, I rejoice and share my joy with you all.* In Romans 12:1, we read, *Therefore I urge you, brethren, by the mercies of God, to present your bodies a living and holy sacrifice, acceptable to God, which is your spiritual service of worship.*

There is another beautiful picture that Christians are supposed to *appear as lights in the world* (Philippians 2:15). The New International Version uses the wording, *Then you will shine among them like stars in the sky* (Philippians 2:15).

The Christian life is intended to be like a star in the universe.

We know that when God created the sun, the moon, and the stars, they were intended to give light on the earth. The Christian life is intended to be like a star in the universe. We are to bring light to our world. When we enter a room, it should be a little brighter!

Jesus used the same figure of speech in talking about Himself: *While I am in the world, I am the Light of the world* (John 9:5). When Jesus came into the world, the light began to shine. The world saw the light like it had never seen it before. It is no wonder that demons were revealed everywhere Jesus traveled. When He returned to heaven, He said it was our responsibility to be the light of the world.

This chapter is written to inspire us to be like "stars in the universe," like diamonds radiating on a black silk canvas. The qualities of being like stars in the universe should challenge us to shine like never before.

OUR LIGHT ENLIGHTENS OTHERS.

The first quality about light is that it simply shines. Paul said, *among whom you appear as lights in the world* (Philippians 2:15). Paul also gave us some things that hinder our light: *Do all things without grumbling or disputing* (Philippians 2:14).

Throughout the Book of Philippians, Paul sprinkled the great thought of joy and rejoicing. The Philippian church was his joy and his crown; but we must remember that as great a church as it was, it was not a perfect church.

As mentioned previously, there were some problems beginning to emerge at the church in Philippi. Paul would deal specifically with those problems in Chapter 4, but what he was trying to do first was cut those problems at the roots. There was some grumbling and disputing that was beginning to move among the congregation. Those are the kinds of things that will hinder the light from shining the way it is intended to shine.

Grumbling is a behind-the-scenes murmuring.

When we think about light in our day, we think about electric lighting; consequently, we have to put ourselves back into the New Testament era in order to get the full picture. In those days, light was created from oils and types of fuels. In the Tabernacle and later in the Temple, there was a lampstand that was fueled by oil. The priests would light the wick in the oil, and it would begin to shine. However, if some impurities got into that wick, they had to trim those impurities out because the smoke would cause the light to be diminished.

Paul was talking about some elements that hinder the light and keep the church from being the light for Jesus it should be. We must not allow our individual testimony to be diminished or dimmed from what God wants it to be. We must be willing to *do all things without grumbling or disputing* (Philippians 2:14).

The Greek word for "grumbling" was a term imitating the sound of cooing doves. The picture of the word, the very sound of the word, gave the meaning of the word—a murmur or mutter with muffled undertones.

Parents know what this word sounded like. They tell their children to go to their rooms and study, but their children want to go outside and play. The parents hear the grumbling and ask,

"What did you say?" "Nothing. I didn't say anything," yet there is a definite humming sound coming from them.

Grumbling is a behind-the-scenes murmuring. It was used by the children of Israel in the Old Testament when they came out of Egypt. They had been redeemed by the blood of the lamb and had crossed over the Red Sea on dry ground yet they were hardly into the wilderness experience before they began grumbling. They mumbled and complained and grumbled against the Lord which definitely hindered them.

There should be nothing in our life that would cause people to point to us with blame.

By Paul's using the word *disputing*, we know there were open complaints at the church in Philippi. It all began with grumbling on the inside and continued with disputing or complaining on the outside. That lifestyle is deadly in the fellowship of a church. Since we are children of God who are saved and redeemed by the blood of Jesus Christ, we have every reason to be joyful believers. We must not become one of the mumblers and grumblers in the congregation because it is deadly to the testimony of a church as well as our individual lives.

A wife said to her husband, "When you married me, you told me you would be humbly grateful; but you have now become grumbly hateful." We must not become grumblers and complainers because it hinders the light. God wants us to be joyful, and we have so much for which to be thankful and so much for which to love Jesus. *Do all things without grumbling or disputing* (Philippians 2:14).

Paul wrote about the elements that help the light and told the Philippians to *prove yourselves to be blameless and innocent, children of God above reproach in the midst of a crooked and perverse generation, among whom you appear as lights in the world* (Philippians 2:15). The two phrases, *blameless and innocent* and *above reproach*, help the light to shine.

The word *blameless* does not mean sinless; it means nothing to find fault with. It means our testimony before a lost world—what a lost world sees they look at us as Christians.

There should be nothing in our life that would cause people to point to us with blame or that would hinder our testimony on the job, at school, or wherever we happen to be. Our attitudes, conduct, speech, and the way we live should be blameless before lost people.

Paul also uses the word *innocent* or *harmless* (KJV) which in his day referred to undiluted wine or unalloyed metal—having no impurities. We are to have nothing in our lives that would be less than pure or sincere. Can we say of our ourselves that we are innocent or *harmless*? What are we in our own sight?

Paul also talked about being *above reproach* or *without rebuke* (KJV) which is what we are to be in the eyes of God. If that is the kind of life we are living, then our light will be like stars in the universe.

OUR LIGHT EXPANDS EVERYWHERE.

One of the great qualities of light is that it expands—it shares itself. *Let your light so shine before men, that they may see your good works, and glorify your Father which is in heaven* (Matthew 5:16).

We Are to Overcome Darkness

Light shares itself by overcoming darkness *in the midst of a crooked and perverse generation, among whom you appear as lights in the world* (Philippians 2:15). The best way to get rid of the darkness is to shine a light.

Many people use a nightlight in their bedrooms because it dispels the darkness and allows them to make their way around the room should they need to get up in the middle of the night.

There are many lighthouses on the coasts of our nation. The purpose of the lighthouse was to overcome the darkness so that the ships could come safely into the harbor. Christians are called to be lights in the world like stars in the universe. We are living in a dark world *so we have the prophetic word made more sure, to which you do well to pay attention as to a lamp shining in a dark place* (2 Peter 1:19).

Christians are called to live a straight life in a crooked world.

We are living in a better world scientifically and technologically; however, we are not living in a better world morally and spiritually. We are living in a crooked and perverse world as demonstrated by the complete lack of logic of people's thinking and the crooked lifestyles of many, but Christians are called to live a straight life in a crooked world.

A crooked and perverse generation. The word "perverse" means to be twisted or distorted. Much of secular music is twisted. Singers spew profanity while making millions of dollars by singing what many would call absolute discord and noise.

Filth, profanity, and vulgarity on the pages of a book enable the sale of millions of copies; and the world calls it literature. Comedians tell dirty jokes, and art is often nothing more than what looks like monkeys scratching on a piece of canvas.

It is time that God's people start being light in this cruel, crooked, and perverse world. This world is going to hell at the speed of sound, and it is time that we call people to some sense of sanity and morality.

Those who have gone along with the world's distortions and crookedness have extinguished the light in their lives and are no longer a testimony for the Lord Jesus Christ.

Some people say, "But I work in a terrible place! You wouldn't believe the lifestyles and ungodliness of the people!"

Perhaps that is why they are there—for God to use them as the light of Jesus in a dark place.

We Are to Offer Direction

Light also offers direction. *Holding fast the word of life, so that in the day of Christ I will have reason to glory because I did not run in vain nor toil in vain* (Philippians 2:16). The Christian is pictured as light, but the Bible is also pictured as light. *Your word is a lamp to my feet and a light to my path* (Psalm 119:105) and *the unfolding of Your words gives light* (Psalm 119:130).

We are called to hold forth the Word of life and share with people the direction that the Word of God provides. People do not know which way to go; they have no sense of direction and no longer know what is right and what is wrong. Those who know and believe the Word should hold forth the Word of God like a beacon light, pointing people in the right direction.

Many couples do not know how to have a godly marriage. Others do not know how to build a career. The answers are all found in the pages of the light of the Word of God, the Bible.

In the final analysis, we do not have a darkness problem but a light problem. It is not that the darkness has become stronger but that the light has become weaker. It is not that the darkness has become greater but that the light has become smaller. It is time to turn on the light, and the darkness will flee! When we become like stars in the universe, the darkness will disappear!

OUR LIGHT EXPELS ENERGY.

But even if I am being poured out as a drink offering upon the sacrifice and service of your faith, I rejoice and share my joy with you all (Philippians 2:17). The phrase *poured out as a drink offering* is used to describe the act of self-sacrifice or the willingness of a person to give up their life for the sake of others. The Apostle Paul used this to describe his willingness to expend himself for fellow Christians.

The drink offering was a part of the Jewish practice of pouring out drink offerings over sacrifices. After a priest would sacrifice a lamb, a ram, or a bull, he would pour wine beside the altar. This symbolized the dedication of a person in worship to God. The drink offering consisted of wine which was poured out on the altar along with the animal sacrifice, and it made a "sweet aroma" to the Lord.

We do not shine unless we burn.

In our modern day of electricity, it is somewhat difficult for us to understand the way they lived in Bible days; but in those days, if a light was to shine, it had to give itself up—burn itself out. By the very nature of its burning, self-sacrifice was involved. When stars shine, they expel energy in order to give forth light.

Jesus used this in talking about John the Baptist: *He was the lamp that was burning and was shining and you were willing to rejoice for a while in his light* (John 5:35). The point was that we do not shine unless we burn. There is a cost to pay. There is a sacrifice to be made to be a light for the Lord Jesus.

In this lies one of the greatest problems with "modern Christianity." We have lost the spirit of sacrifice. Many believers think sacrifice is going to church on a rainy Sunday morning. Many others are not old enough to remember regular Sunday night services. When enough Christians stopped coming to the evening services, they were canceled throughout the United States.

When our culture began to turn against Christianity, believers stopped sharing Christ. The buzz word among so many was "share your faith." However, nowhere in the New Testament are we taught to share our faith; instead, we are taught to share Christ. Our faith cannot save; only Christ can save. This is more than semantics. Jesus is the light of the world!

Upon the sacrifice and service of your faith (Philippians 2:17). Sacrifice and service go together. All effective light giving—service for Jesus—involves sacrifice. In our day, however, most people prefer convenience over sacrifice. Nevertheless, sacrifice is always involved in effective service. Service without sacrifice is activity rather than ministry. Some people just get involved in activity, but ministry comes when we learn to sacrifice—to give of ourselves.

Are we useful Christians? Are we shining for the Lord Jesus Christ? Are we like stars in the universe? *But even if I am being poured out as a drink offering upon the sacrifice and service of your faith, I rejoice and share my joy with you all* (Philippians 2:17). Paul said that when we are poured out as a drink offering, we will not only be useful but also joyful.

In Philippians 2:17-18, Paul uses the words *joy* or *rejoice* several times. He was teaching that people who learn to sacrifice for Jesus, let their lights shine, and sacrifice in order that their lights will shine, learn that it brings great joy in their lives.

Many people think the whole point of life is just accumulating "stuff." If only they can accumulate more gadgets, more accolades, and more activities in their lives, they will be happy. However, the Bible says that the way to be happy is not to add to your life but to give your life.

The mother and father who are willing to give of themselves and pour into the life of their child are the mother and father who find joy. The person who learns to find real joy in marriage is not the one who comes into the marriage saying, "What is this marriage going to do for me?" but the one who comes into the marriage saying, "How much can I give of myself?"

Light shines. Light shares. Light sacrifices. Light overcomes darkness. Light offers direction in a darkened world. As we burn, we begin to shine for Jesus. No bleeding—no blessing. No cost—no consecration. No willingness to give—no wealth to others.

Henry Martyn arrived in India in 1806; and until his death in 1812, he translated the whole of the New Testament into Urdu,

Persian and Judaeo-Persic. He also translated the Psalms into Persian and the Book of Common Prayer into Urdu. Prior to his death, he was heard to say, "Let me burn out for God," an indication of his zeal for the things of God.

Find that place of service to be a light in this dark world.

Adoniram Judson arrived in Burma in 1812 and worked there for almost forty years. Judson was one of the first Protestant missionaries to Burma. He translated the Bible into Burmese and established a number of churches in Burma. He labored for seven years before he baptized his first convert. He went through illness, loneliness, and the death of his baby boy in addition to being in prison for two years for preaching the gospel. His beloved wife, Ann, and his daughter, Maria, both died of spotted fever; but Adoniram Judson said, "I will not leave Burma until the cross of Christ is planted here forever." Thirty years after the death of Adoniram Judson, there were 63 churches and 7,000 converts in Burma because he was willing to give of himself. He lit up his world.

God wants all of us to find that place of service to be a light in this dark world. Whether it be in a profession or on a mission field or in an office or a neighborhood, we must find the place God wants us to be and make up our minds that we are going to light up our personal and professional worlds. Then we must let our light shine brightly. We can be like the stars in the universe!

12

PASSING JOY TO OTHERS

In a rather interesting manner, Paul explains to us what joy is really all about in this life. J.O.Y. JOY. If we want to have joy in our life, we must put Jesus first. That is the "J." Put others second. That is the "O." Put "yourself" last. That is the "Y." When it is in that order, it spells "JOY."

In Philippians 1, the emphasis is upon the Lord Jesus, and we find repeatedly that Paul emphasized Jesus, exalted Jesus, and put Jesus first in his life.

In Philippians 2, we discover that the emphasis turns to others. The emphasis is upon living our life for others in order to have a joyful and fulfilled life. Paul began by giving the greatest illustration of all—that of someone who lived for others—none other than the Lord Jesus Christ Himself. *Do not merely look out for your own personal interests, but also for the interests of others* (Philippians 2:4).

As we move through Philippians 2, we discover that Paul began to use illustrations of people with whom we can identify.

One of these was a young man named Timothy. *I hope in the Lord Jesus to send Timothy to you shortly* (Philippians 2:19).

Timothy was a great example of a powerful believer and what it meant to be a Christian. Paul told Timothy to *let no one look down on your youthfulness, but rather in speech, conduct, love, faith and purity, show yourself an example of those who believe* (1 Timothy 4:12).

We are only one generation away from paganism in our churches, in our nation, and in our world.

There are many young people who have influenced Christian history. Martin Luther was only 33 years of age when he nailed his *Ninety-Five Theses* to the door of All Saints' Church, Wittenberg, Germany, in 1517 and started the Protestant Reformation. Billy Graham was only 30 when he conducted the now-famous Los Angeles crusade in September 1949 which launched his career as the greatest evangelist in the history of the Christian faith. Many of the great Christians in the pages of church history were young people who were on fire for Christ.

Young people are a vital link in the gospel chain. It is through young people as they carry on the message of the Lord that the good news of Jesus goes forth. Paul told Timothy that *the things which you have heard from me in the presence of many witnesses, entrust these to faithful men who will be able to teach others also* (2 Timothy 2:2). Paul was telling Timothy that just as we have been taught by others, we must in turn teach others. The gospel chain goes from link to link, from generation to generation. We must understand the importance of shaping and molding young people in order to carry forward the gospel of Jesus Christ because we are only one generation away from paganism in our churches, in our nation, and in our world.

Movements often become monuments and usually wind up being the opposite of what they started out to be. Passion becomes apathy and inspiration becomes indifference because throughout the last 2,000 years, the Church failed at some point to raise up a new generation of Bible-based, faith-fortified, Spirit-filled servants to impact their generation.

The first generation generates, the second generation motivates, the third generation speculates, and the fourth generation dissipates. The only way out of a decline is up. The only way to stop the erosion of our evangelism is to raise up young champions for Christ.

Paul wrote about a young man who was a young preacher. I can identify with what that means as the Lord called me to preach when I was a 14-year-old boy, the most unlikely person in the world to become a preacher; and I preached my first sermon at the age of 18. There are some things about Timothy that will encourage us about young people as well as encourage young people also.

WE ARE SONS.

That which was true of Timothy should be true of every young person and of all of us. Timothy was Paul's son in the Lord and wrote the Philippians concerning him saying, *But you know of his proven worth, that he served with me in the furtherance of the gospel like a child serving his father* (Philippians 2:22).

We Are Shaped

Timothy's background emerges in Acts 16. Timothy was shaped by his family just as all of us are products of our family backgrounds. What we are, most of what we think, and many of the things we do are influenced by the kind of family we had. Family is extremely important because it molds and shapes the lives of its children and young people.

A sad commentary on the life of many of our young people is reflected by a young woman who said, "Why do I need a home? I was born in a hospital, educated in a college, engaged in a car, and married in a hotel. I eat out of a grocery store and paper bags and spend my mornings on a golf course, my afternoons at a bridge table, and my evenings at the movies. When I die, I'm going to be buried in a cemetery. All I need is a garage."

God can take a minus and turn it into a positive.

Timothy had a "minus" in his family background because his father was not a believer in Christ. There are many people in the same situation who have a minus in their families. Their dads are not saved—perhaps their moms are not either. Maybe they are the only person in their family who knows Christ as Savior. They attend church alone, and their families could care less. They need to be encouraged that they may be the one God can use to bring their whole family to know Christ as Savior. We must live for Jesus in front of them and show them that Christ can make a difference in their lives. They can be a witness to the members of their family and hopefully win their brothers and sisters to the Lord as well as their own mom or dad. God can take a minus and turn it into a positive.

There was also a plus in Timothy's family because he had a Christian grandmother and a Christian mother. Because of them, Timothy was a saved son with a wonderful heritage! Anyone who has a Christian father, mother, or grandparent has much for which to be thankful. Paul said, *I am mindful of the sincere faith within you, which first dwelt in your grandmother Lois and your mother Eunice* (2 Timothy 1:5). Timothy could look at his grandmother and his mother and see a faith that was genuine.

Do our children see a genuine faith when they look at us? Do our grandchildren see a Christian testimony? Young people are often turned off to the church and Christianity because of the inconsistencies they see in their parents. They observe their unfaithfulness to the house of God and say, "If it doesn't mean anything to them, then why should it mean anything to me?"

Young people are often turned off to the church and Christianity because of the inconsistencies they see in their parents.

Timothy had a great advantage because of the Christian background of his grandmother and mother; but in and of itself, that was not enough. It is true that his family background helped mold his life, but something had to happen in Timothy's life in order for him to master his life as well as he did.

Having godly family members does not automatically save a person. There must be a personal experience with Jesus Christ. As we put the pieces of Timothy's background together, we discover in Acts 16 that Paul came to his city. God was orchestrating circumstances whereby Paul would be placed in Timothy's path. Would to God that all parents would take their children to the house of the Lord so that they might be exposed to pastors and preachers. When I was young, my parents taught us to love preachers. I loved my pastors who preached the Word to me. I love pastors and preachers today who faithfully preach and teach God's Word.

We Are Saved

It would seem that Timothy came to faith during Paul's first missionary journey. As Paul preached the gospel of Jesus Christ, the Holy Spirit took the message of the Word and Timothy gave his heart to Jesus.

How was Timothy saved? Just like every person is saved . . . by realizing they are a sinner and that Jesus died on the cross for their sins and by repenting of their sins and inviting Jesus personally to come into their heart and life and be their personal Savior. Timothy became a son in the faith—a child of God.

However, it was not until Paul's second missionary journey that he took Timothy along with him (Acts 16:1-3). For many years, Timothy accompanied Paul, experienced danger with him, and served him faithfully.

We Are Seasoned

Timothy was not only *shaped* and *saved*, but he was also *seasoned*. I can almost imagine that when Paul came back, he heard others exclaim: "Have you heard about Eunice's young son, Timothy? He is just an amazing person and is growing by leaps and bounds and maturing in the Lord. God is going to do great things in his life!"

God had His hands on Timothy, and Paul gave him time to mature and develop. The same is true of young people today. We must be careful not to put young people in a position when they are not ready but rather allow God to mold and shape them and get them ready for where He will send them in the future.

Paul urged Timothy not to have a spirit of timidity but a spirit of power, love, and discipline and not to be ashamed of the testimony of the Lord but retain the sound words through which Paul trained him and guard through the Holy Spirit the treasure that had been entrusted to him (1 Timothy 1:7-14). These are the same things we must *season* in our young people.

WE ARE TO BE SERVANTS.

But you know of his proven worth, that he served with me in the furtherance of the gospel like a child serving his father (Philippians 2:22). Timothy was called to preach and called to be a servant of the Lord. God still calls young people to serve

Him and to step out in faith and do what God would have them to do. God has a plan and purpose for every life.

We Have a Calling

God called Timothy to be a preacher of the gospel of the Lord Jesus Christ and gave him a concern for others. *But I hope in the Lord Jesus to send Timothy to you shortly, so that I also may be encouraged when I learn of your condition* (Philippians 2:19). Paul then told why he was sending Timothy: *For I have no one else of kindred spirit who will genuinely be concerned for your welfare* (Philippians 2:20). Paul was telling them that Timothy had a soul equal to his—he had the same heartbeat and was interested in and willing to serve others.

The Church will not have enough ministers to complete the Great Commission.

Paul then made a great indictment: *For they all seek after their own interests, not those of Christ Jesus* (Philippians 2:21). He was saying that everyone around there was watching out for themselves with little concern for the things of Jesus.

For too long, the Western Church has watered down the calling of God of the laying on of hands to young people and their call into the ministry. It became fashionable to turn bible colleges into Christian universities with the belief that just as many would be trained for ministry. How mistaken that decision was. We do not train God-called ministers the same way we train doctors, lawyers, teachers, and business leaders. Over the last 20 years, this training approach has netted less, not more, young people being trained for fulltime ministry. In numerous denominations, there are not enough God-called young people "in the pipeline" to carry the Western Church forward with fire in the future.

One of the fastest growing crises is that the Church will not have enough ministers to complete the Great Commission at the current rate of training young people for ministry. With this stark reality in mind, the Global Church Network launched the Million Ministers Mandate several years ago. As we move forward, every Global Church Network Hub should have at least 40 percent of their attendees between the ages of 15 and 35. Additionally, the Global Church Divinity School (www.GCDS.tv) was developed to help turn every member into a missionary and every church into a seminary. In the next ten years, we believe it is possible for at least one million young ministers to be called, equipped, and sent into fulltime ministry!

We Are to Be Concerned

Paul needed someone to go to Philippi, someone he could count on—a servant spirit. As he went down his list, however, he said, "No, I can't count on him. No, I couldn't send him. She could have gone but wouldn't. No, they're too wrapped up in themselves."

I have also had a list through the years. When it came time to pick people to do certain things, to serve in certain capacities, I would go over the list and say, "Can I count on this one? Will this one work? They are capable and have the ability and the gifts. They could be so effective, but I can't count on them. I don't even know if they are going to show up or if they are willing to pay the price."

We are in one of two verses in Philippians: 1:21—*For to me, to live is Christ and to die is gain* or 2:21—*For they all seek after their own interests, not those of Christ Jesus.* Where does Jesus fit into our plans and activities? Where does He fit into the way we arrange our priorities? Are we totally committed to Christ?

Paul said Timothy was a servant with a genuine concern for other people. *For I have no man likeminded, who will naturally care for your state* (Philippians 2:20 KJV). In terms of our own natural condition, we really do not care about people; but the word *naturally* means a birthright. Paul was talking about what had come into Timothy's life because of his new birth experience. Because Timothy had been born again, he *naturally*, by his birth, cared for others. Consequently, Timothy not only cared for people *naturally* but also supernaturally.

Timothy was Paul's substitute.

God has to teach us to care for people and create a love in our hearts for them. God has to give us a servant spirit. Timothy was called, and he was concerned.

We Are to Cooperate

But you know of his proven worth, that he served with me in the furtherance of the gospel like a child serving his father (Philippians 2:22). Paul was Timothy's spiritual father, not his physical father. Timothy was Paul's son in the faith; Timothy was in the "family business."

In contrasting Paul and Timothy, Paul was an old man; Timothy a young man. Paul was a full-blooded Jew; Timothy a half-breed. Paul was bold; Timothy perhaps rather timid. However, they were in cooperation, serving together. The key: *He served with me in the furtherance of the gospel.* That is what puts generations together.

WE ARE TO BE A SUBSTITUTE.

What Paul said about Timothy should be said of us, "He is a son, a servant." *I hope in the Lord Jesus to send Timothy to you shortly* (Philippians 2:19). Timothy was Paul's substitute: "I am sending him in my place." Timothy was constantly willing to be sent out—to Corinth, to Thessalonica, to Philippi; and Timothy was evidently willing to go anywhere, help anyone no matter who they were, and sacrifice anything. *But ye know the proof of him* (Philippians 2:22 KJV). The word *proof* is a word that was used for the melting down of ore. It meant to be put to the test. Paul said of Timothy, "He has been through the fire and is willing to sacrifice anything to be a substitute, to be a sent one, to go for God, and to go for me." Are we willing to go anywhere Jesus wants us to go, serve anyone He wants us to serve, and sacrifice anything He wants us to sacrifice? If we are not a witness for Jesus where we live, what makes us think a trip elsewhere is going to make a missionary out of us?

To find God's will, to follow God's will, and to finish God's will.

Timothy later became a pastor who was greatly used of God. The Apostle Paul wrote two letters to Timothy; and in the last letter we have record of, he said, *Make every effort to come before winter* (2 Timothy 4:21).

Is God saying to us, "I want you to go"? Are we ready and willing? Is He saying, *Come before winter*? In other words, do not delay but come now. Come while we are able. Come during this season of life.

When I was 13 years old, God called me into full-time evangelistic ministry; and I began traveling and preaching when I was 18. During that same timeframe, my brother, James L.; Mike Bagwell; and I devised a plan to knock on every door in the city of Mobile, Alabama. I still have a copy of the simple brochure we wanted to give to people who answered their door. We mapped out neighborhoods long before Google devised a much simpler way. For months and months on Sunday afternoons, the three of us would knock on doors and share Christ with strangers. Why? Because people were lost and most times did not even know it. Why? Because Christ moved our hearts to reach out to the best of our ability to the least, the last, and the lost. Why? Because if we could be faithful with the "little things," our Lord could trust us with the bigger things.

Many years have transpired since my brother, Mike, and I shared the gospel together. I lost contact with Mike; but my brother and I continue to run the only race that matters: to find God's will, to follow God's will, and to finish God's will.

Come before winter! Make a decision today to follow Christ and fulfill His divine destiny in your life!

13

KNOCKING ON DEATH'S DOOR FOR CHRIST

Throughout the Book of Philippians as well as in other New Testament books Paul wrote, it is obvious that he was constantly thinking about others. Paul devoted himself to the Lord Jesus Christ and the development of deep friendships. He not only knew how to win souls but also how to win friends. Romans 16 lists at least 35 names of people who were friends of Paul.

Epaphroditus, whose name means very lovely or handsome and charming, is mentioned in Philippians 2:25 and 4:18. He is a picture of a consecrated layperson who gave himself totally and unreservedly to the service of the Lord. He is immortalized in Scripture because he was willing to "lay it all on the line" for Jesus.

Epaphroditus was one of those selfless Christians who did not have to be the quarterback on the team or the big fish in a little pond. He was willing to accept the role to which God called him and serve the Lord with devotion. Epaphroditus's story can certainly bring to mind fellow servants we know in the body of Christ who have given their all to fulfill God's will for their lives.

What does it mean to "lay it all on the line" for Christ? What does it look like when a Christian goes the extra mile, beyond the call of duty?

WE ARE TO BE STABLE CHRISTIANS.

But I thought it necessary to send to you Epaphroditus, my brother and fellow worker and fellow soldier, who is also your messenger and minister to my need (Philippians 2:25). Epaphroditus was Paul's brother in the Lord, his coworker, and his fellow soldier in Christ—a picture of a balanced Christian.

We are not to become gospel sheriffs.

There is a tendency for churches and Christians to get out of balance or become unstable. Some become like a wobbly tire because they go to extremes in certain directions and never learn the value of balance. How is a Christian to live in a stable manner?

In Philippians 1, Paul talks about our *fellowship* in the gospel (v.5), the *furtherance* of the gospel (v.12), and striving together for the *faith* of the gospel (v.27). These three phrases identify the balance that Christ intends us to have as believers. Our *fellowship* in the gospel is sharing the things of Christ together. The *furtherance* of the gospel means winning other people to faith in Christ in order to spread the gospel. Striving together for the *faith* is standing for the Lord like a good soldier.

Many have a tendency to get these three areas out of balance. If we are not careful, we can become so interested in the fellowship of the gospel that it becomes the total circumference of our ministry. Or we can become so interested in the furtherance of the gospel and winning people to faith in Christ that we do not grow and develop personally in discipleship to become the kind of Christian God desires. Or we can get so involved in fighting for the faith that we become a theological fighter—so earnestly contending for the faith that we become contentious. We are not to become gospel sheriffs.

We must not develop an ingrown attitude in our Christian life.

Epaphroditus was a balanced and stable Christian whom Paul called *my brother*, one with whom he shared the fellowship of the gospel. Paul had previously spoken about Timothy who was his son in the faith; consequently, Paul, Timothy, and Epaphroditus were in the same family, shared the same Savior, and had been saved by the same grace.

Epaphroditus was also Paul's *companion in labour* (KJV). There can be no doubt Epaphroditus was involved in seeking the furtherance of the gospel and was a soulwinner and a witness for the Lord. As wonderful as the fellowship of the gospel is and as much as we enjoy the people of God, we must not develop an ingrown attitude in our Christian life.

Epaphroditus was also Paul's fellow soldier. We are in a battle; the Christian life is not a playground but a battleground. We are to endure hardness as good soldiers of Jesus Christ and fight the good fight of faith. God's people must take their stand and get on the front lines of the battle for truth, morality, and decency in our nation.

WE ARE TO BE SACRIFICIAL CHRISTIANS.

Epaphroditus is not only a stable Christian but also a sacrificial Christian. He *longed after you all, and was full of heaviness, because that ye had heard that he* [Epaphroditus] *had been sick* (Philippians 2:26 KJV). We know that the Book of Philippians is a book of Christian joy in the Lord; however, we may be a bit surprised to find that Paul uses words such as *heaviness* and speaks of *sorrow upon sorrow* (Philippians 2:27). Sometimes the "highway of happiness" leads us through the "valley of sorrow."

Illnesses come to God's people for many reasons.

The words *full of heaviness* carry the idea of mental and emotional anguish. It is the same words that were used of Jesus in the Garden of Gethsemane. It is a picture that means not at home or a sense of estrangement. In the Garden of Gethsemane, Christ was exceedingly sorrowful. Epaphroditus was also filled with mental and emotional anguish. He had his own personal Gethsemane.

Sooner or later, most Christians also have their own Gethsemane. There are times of happiness, *a time to laugh* (Ecclesiastes 3:4), and times of heaviness, *a time to weep* (Ecclesiastes 3:4). In our churches, we often focus on the joyful element but forget there is also a sorrowful element.

The worldliness of the average congregation of our day should be a source of sorrow to us and cause us to weep. The lack of commitment on the part of many of God's people who own a religion of convenience should cause us to weep. When we look at our own hearts and our own failings, it should cause us to weep. There is a time for *heaviness* in the house of the Lord.

The reason Epaphroditus was full of heaviness was because he was sick and did not want to cause anguish to those in the church at Philippi. Paul adds that *indeed he was sick to the point of death, but God had mercy on him, and not on him only but also on me, so that I would not have sorrow upon sorrow* (Philippians 2:27). We learn from Paul the reason Epaphroditus was in Rome:

I have received everything in full and have an abundance; I am amply supplied, having received from Epaphroditus what you have sent, a fragrant aroma, an acceptable sacrifice, well-pleasing to God (Philippians 4:18).

Epaphroditus was evidently a layman in the church at Philippi, and the church had sent a gift to Paul through him. Epaphroditus stayed for a period of time to minister to Paul's needs; and while he was there, he became ill. But why did he become ill? He was right in the middle of faithful service. He was totally committed and sold out to the Lord Jesus Christ yet he had a time of serious illness. Illnesses come to God's people for many reasons.

Dissipation

Sometimes sickness is because of **dissipation**. Some are sick because they overeat. Some are sick because they abuse their bodies. Some are sick because they do not get enough rest. We sometimes become ill because of our dissipation.

Discipline

At other times we become ill because of **discipline**. Perhaps God is doing a work in our life. Perhaps God is dealing with something in our life that needs and permits a time of illness. Sometimes sickness comes because God is trying to develop us, and sickness is one of the tools He uses.

There are many who are currently going through sickness and testing. God honors us by the size of the test He gives us. Consider Abraham and Lot. Lot pitched his tent toward Sodom, and the temptation of Sodom was almost his undoing.

God tested Abraham by having him put his son, Isaac, on the altar. There are little tests for little faith and big tests for big faith. If God had tried to test Lot like He tested Abraham, it would be like trying to shoot mosquitoes with atom bombs.

Epaphroditus longed *for you all* [the church at Philippi] *and was distressed because you had heard that he was sick* (Philippians

2:26). What burdened Epaphroditus was not so much that he was sick but that the church was burdened because they had heard he was sick. Such unselfishness on the part of Epaphroditus.

Most of the time when we become ill, we get caught up in ourselves. In fact, some believers seem to "enjoy" poor health. It is best not to ask them how they are feeling because we will receive a full "organ recital" of their pains.

Every time we give, we have a part in missions.

Not Epaphroditus. He was concerned for his **church.** With the rise of Internet streaming, it seems we are raising a generation of pajama Christians who rarely get up, get dressed, and go to the local church. If we love our church, we will want to attend and fellowship with our brothers and sisters in Christ.

Epaphroditus was also concerned for **missions.** He had apparently laid his job aside and taken the gift which the believers in Philippi were sending to the Apostle Paul. Epaphroditus became personally involved in missions. Every time we give, we have a part in missions. Although we often pray for missions, perhaps we should also consider whether God would have us lay down what we are doing for a few years and go to the mission field and tell a lost world about the Lord Jesus Christ.

Epaphroditus was also burdened for the **lost.** Although *he was sick to the point of death* (Philippians 2:27), he did not regard his own life.

Rome was the common sink of all of the worst vices of the empire. The dregs and the depths of human depravity could be found in the slums of Rome. In that day, there was a special group of people called the *Parabolini*, those who risked their lives to minister to the sick by exposing themselves to contagious diseases. They would bury the dead and do it at great risk to their personal health. The word literally means to toss the dice. It is a picture of people who were willing to literally gamble their lives in order to be a witness for the Lord.

Christian leaders like Epaphroditus were *men who have risked their lives for the name of our Lord Jesus Christ* (Acts 15:26). Paul spoke of those *who for my life risked their own necks, to whom not only do I give thanks, but also all the churches of the Gentiles* (Romans 16:4). They put their necks on the line.

Epaphroditus hazarded his life for the gospel and for the Apostle Paul. Unfortunately, we are living in a day of convenience. People want church to be convenient. They will only attend when it is not inconvenient. The service must not be too long, and the preacher must preach an encouraging sermon and make them feel good.

As believers, however, we must not rob people of the truth of the gospel of Christ. We must not lower the standard for anyone but keep it exactly where God set it. We must call people to a total commitment to Christ, to lay it all on the line for the Lord. When we sell out to Jesus is when the blessings come.

WE ARE TO BE SIGNIFICANT CHRISTIANS.

Epaphroditus was not only a stable and sacrificial Christian but also a significant Christian. We must make up our minds not to go through life without being a blessing to others. The last zero in 1,000,000,000 has the most value in the billion. The closer we move to the front, the more we decrease our value. If we do not mind being the last zero, we can add compounding value to everyone else.

Epaphroditus was a blessed Christian, and he blessed Paul by bringing him the gift from the church at Philippi and then staying in Rome and ministering for a time. He was a valuable friend to Paul.

Epaphroditus was also significant to the believers in Philippi for Paul said, *Therefore I have sent him all the more eagerly so that when you see him again you may rejoice and I may be less concerned about you* (Philippians 2:28). When people see us coming, do they rejoice or do they say, "Oh, my gracious, here comes Mr. Gripe." "Oh no, here comes Sister Bellyacher." "I cannot believe it, but here comes Critic Charlie, Sarcastic Sally, and Negative Norman." Do we light up a room or make it darker? Are people refreshed or worn out by our presence? Undoubtedly, the Philippian church said, "We look forward to seeing Epaphroditus come back."

We should desire that our lives have a rippling effect on earth and in heaven.

Even 2,000 years after he died, Epaphroditus is still being a blessing. We read about him and are renewed in our spirits and souls. This is the kind of person we should all aspire to be. We should desire that our lives have a rippling effect on earth and in heaven. We need to be stable, sacrificial, and significant.

THE PRIZE OF THE CHRISTIAN LIFE
(PHILIPPIANS 3:1-21)

14

THE GREAT EXCHANGE

¹Finally, my brethren, rejoice in the Lord. To write the same things again is no trouble to me, and it is a safeguard for you. ²Beware of the dogs, beware of the evil workers, beware of the false circumcision; ³for we are the true circumcision, who worship in the Spirit of God and glory in Christ Jesus and put no confidence in the flesh, ⁴although I myself might have confidence even in the flesh. If anyone else has a mind to put confidence in the flesh, I far more: ⁵circumcised the eighth day, of the nation of Israel, of the tribe of Benjamin, a Hebrew of Hebrews; as to the Law, a Pharisee; ⁶as to zeal, a persecutor of the church; as to the righteousness which is in the Law, found blameless. ⁷But whatever things were gain to me, those things I have counted as loss for the sake of Christ. ⁸More than that, I count all things to be loss in view of the surpassing value of knowing Christ Jesus my Lord, for whom I have suffered the loss of all things, and count them but rubbish so that

I may gain Christ, ⁹and may be found in Him, not having a righteousness of my own derived from the Law, but that which is through faith in Christ, the righteousness which comes from God on the basis of faith (Philippians 3:1-9).

In Philippians 3:7-8, Paul is talking about the things that really matter in life. Many people—even church people—are spending time and energy on things that do not really count. A thousand or a million years from now, they will make absolutely no difference. We each need a checkup to see if we are living a life that really counts.

We each need a checkup to see if we are living a life that really counts.

If it is a life of legalism, then it is not a life that counts. The Apostle Paul had lived that life and had had enough of it. The Lord Jesus Christ met him on the Damascus Road and saved and transformed him. He would then go on to fight legalism with every ounce of his strength for the rest of his life.

Paul began with a warning: *Beware of dogs . . . beware of evil workers . . . of the false circumcision* (Philippians 3:2). Who were the *dogs*? The legalists—the Judaizers, those who attacked Paul, would say, "You're not saved just by believing in Jesus. You must keep the Law of Moses and perform certain rituals and ceremonies." In using such strong language as *Beware of dogs*, Paul was characterizing false religious teachers not as "house pets" but as cruel, vicious, snapping, snarling, barking, biting, filthy alley dogs.

Paul was saying that some of the meanest people are in the world of religion; consequently, we must *beware*. We must not think that just because people are religious that they are necessarily "nice" for it was the religious crowd that crucified Jesus.

When Paul said, *beware of the concision* (Philippians 3:2 KJV), he was saying to call it by its true name: mutilation. The legalists were the ones who were always preaching circumcision, but Paul called them mutilators and said that legalism could save no one. Religiosity aside, a person must be born again in order to be saved. Religion without Jesus Christ is hopeless because religion can save no one. Religion without righteousness is repugnant to God.

It is often harder to reach a religious person for Jesus than a hardened sinner.

It is often harder to reach a religious person for Jesus than a hardened sinner. This is the reason why Jesus, in looking at the Pharisees who were the religionists, said, *Truly I say to you that the tax collectors and prostitutes will get into the kingdom of God before you. For John came to you in the way of righteousness and you did not believe him; but the tax collectors and prostitutes did believe him; and you, seeing this, did not even feel remorse afterward so as to believe him* (Matthew 21:31-32).

So many in our nation are egomaniacs strutting their way to hell, thinking they are too good to be damned. They do not understand that they must be born again because they believe they are "nice" people. Self-righteousness is very deceptive. Paul was warning them and showing them that religion alone could not save them, that legalism could not save them, and that ritualism could not save them.

Paul opened the book of his own life. His life before Christ was bankrupt in spite of all of his religion; but after he gave his life to the Lord, he found he was immensely wealthy.

THE OLD MATH OF LIFE

I myself might have confidence even in the flesh (Philippians 3:4). When he was talking about confidence in the flesh, he was addressing those things people depend upon to earn human merit or achievement for their salvation. Paul was dealing with those who were bragging about how good they were and said, "If you want to get into a bragging contest, then I'll get into one with you. You think you've got something to boast about? I've got more to boast about than any of you!" Paul then went on to tell the things he could boast about in the flesh.

Our Rituals

Paul said he was *circumcised the eighth day* (Philippians 3:5). The ritual of circumcision was performed on him when he was only eight days old. He was very aware of the ritual.

There are many people who believe that just being a good person is enough to attain eternal life while others talk about how they were sprinkled or baptized as a child. They believe a little water is enough to save them. Baptism, whether a spoonful or a tankful, cannot take anyone to heaven.

Our Relationships

Not only did Paul have ritual, but he also had the pride of relationship. *Circumcised the eighth day, of the nation of Israel* (Philippians 3:5). Paul's family tree was respectable; he came from Jewish aristocrats. However, he discovered that God has no grandchildren—only children. Even if our parents are right with God, that does not make us right with God.

Our Respectability

Paul was a man who not only had pride of ritual and pride of relationship, but he also had pride of respectability for he was *of the tribe of Benjamin* (Philippians 3:5). The tribe of Benjamin was a great tribe! When the other tribes went astray, Benjamin did not. Israel's first king came from the tribe of Benjamin that had *700 choice men* [who] *were left-handed; each one could sling a stone at a hair and not miss* (Judges 20:16). They were the elite, the special troops of the children of Israel. *After thee, O Benjamin* (Hosea 5:8 KJV) seemed to have become a war cry of the tribe. Yet Paul was saying, "I don't care how respectable you are. You may be held in high regard, but you're still just as lost as a bootlegger if you've not come to the Lord Jesus Christ."

It was not race—but grace—that got a person into heaven.

Our Race

In addition, Paul had the pride of race as *a Hebrew of Hebrews* (Philippians 3:5). He could have said, "I'm as pure as it gets. There is no gentile blood in my family. We didn't take on the ways of the Greeks. There is no Hellenist in our family. We're pure. We've kept all the rituals. I am a Hebrew of Hebrews." He had pride of race but found that it was not race—but grace—that got a person into heaven.

Our Religion

Paul was not finished. He said, "Now if you want to brag, I can brag." He had pride in religion *as to the Law, a Pharisee* (Philippians 3:5). The Pharisees were the strictest sect—the most orthodox, and Paul was intensely orthodox. He had zeal and defended his religion by persecuting the Church. There were approximately 6,000 Pharisees in the first century.

Our Reputation

There was the pride of reputation—*as to zeal, a persecutor of the church; as to the righteousness which is in the Law, found blameless* (Philippians 3:6). Zeal was considered to be one of the finest characteristics of religious life. When we read the record of

Paul before he came to know Christ as his Savior, we can see the level of his zealousness. He was so zealous he would kill anyone who disagreed with him.

Those who followed Paul would have said, "My, what a good man!" He was not sinless and knew he was not, but he said, "I am blameless—not sinless in the eyes of God but blameless in the eyes of men." No one could have pointed a finger at him and said, "He's a thief," or "He's a liar," or "He's a pervert," or "He's an adulterer."

We could conclude that if religion could get a person into heaven, then religion certainly would have gotten Paul into heaven. Yet he said, *But whatever things were gain to me, those things I have counted as loss for the sake of Christ* (Philippians 3:7). When he looked at all of the accoutrements and all of the wealth, it was zero—a total loss. Good works do not and cannot save.

For Paul, everything was a total loss. Whatever things he had gained did not make him godlier or bring him to Christ. So many people think they can be saved by doing good works—their own self-righteousness, and these are the hardest people to reach because they are satisfied—they are *good people*.

One of the first things a man might say regarding a relationship with Christ could be, "But I'm a moral person. I live a good life. I'm a good father to my children and a great husband to my wife." All of that is admirable, but a person can be morally good in terms of the outward keeping of the commandments of God. There may be nothing anyone can accuse them of, yet they are still not saved.

THE NEW MATH WITH THE LORD

Whatever things were gain to me—all the things in the credit column—*those things I have counted as loss for the sake of Christ* (Philippians 3:7) Something happened to Paul. Something took place which changed his method of mathematics. *More than that, I count all things to be loss in view of the surpassing value of knowing Christ Jesus my Lord, for whom I have suffered the loss of all things, and count them but rubbish so that I may gain Christ, and may be found in Him, not having a righteousness of my own derived from the Law, but that which is through faith in Christ, the righteousness which comes from God on the basis of faith* (Philippians 3:8-9).

Even a good thing is a bad thing if it becomes a substitute for the best thing.

Paul was on the road to Damascus—on his way to persecute believers in Jesus. He was a religious man, a zealous man, a sincere man. He had the official papers in his hand giving him the right to persecute them, and then something happened that completely changed his method of calculation. Suddenly, everything he had placed in the credit column was instantly moved over into the loss column.

It was just like the stars disappearing before the sun. It was like pasting pearls alongside real diamonds. He discovered that everything he had bragged about and counted as his spiritual wealth was all worthless.

He previously had valued his race, his religion, his self-righteousness, and so much more. In and of themselves, these were not bad. He was not ashamed to be a Hebrew and was grateful to be a Roman citizen, but Paul discovered that even a good thing is a bad thing if it becomes a substitute for the best thing.

What changed his mathematics? When Paul was on the road to Damascus, he was holding on to all the things he had done to earn and merit salvation by human achievement. However, he was confronted by the living Lord Jesus Christ whom he thought was dead. When Jesus died on the cross of Calvary, Paul thought that was the end of the matter.

Perhaps he was in the jeering section at the cross and was glad when they put Jesus in the tomb and sealed it. Then suddenly on the Damascus Road, he made the startling discovery that Jesus Christ was not dead but was alive. Everything Paul had depended upon to save him and to earn and his salvation was for naught.

Suppose a camper takes his backpack which is filled with his canteen, mess kit, food, and blanket and boards a plane to fly to where he intends to go camping. While the plane is in the air, it begins to go down. Rather than grabbing a parachute, the camper grabs his backpack and jumps out of the plane. Obviously, there is nothing wrong with a backpack; however, the camper needed a parachute yet chose a backpack. Because of that, the backpack and his life were a total loss.

Paul said, *Those things I have counted as loss for the sake of Christ.* He was not saying that they were bad in and of themselves. The worst form of badness may be human goodness when human goodness becomes a substitute for the new birth. If Paul had wanted to brag, he would certainly have been able to due to his pedigree as a blueblood and a religionist; but he counted them all as loss that he might gain Christ.

Our Burden for Christ

It was very costly to Paul to come to Christ. It cost him **financial** stability. Paul was likely a fairly well-to-do man or certainly his family was wealthy because he was able to travel all the way from Tarsus to Jerusalem to study under Gamaliel, one of the greatest teachers of the day. Yet when Paul came to Jesus, he became an itinerant preacher who moonlighted as a tentmaker in order to preach the gospel of Christ.

Paul experienced many **fitness** challenges in his ministry: *far more labors, in far more imprisonments, beaten times without number, often in danger of death. Five times I received from the Jews thirty-nine lashes. Three times I was beaten with rods, once I was stoned, three times I was shipwrecked, a night and a day I have spent in the deep. I have been on frequent journeys,* *in dangers from rivers, dangers from robbers, dangers from my countrymen, dangers from the Gentiles, dangers in the city, dangers in the wilderness, dangers on the sea, dangers among false brethren; I have been in labor and hardship, through many sleepless nights, in hunger and thirst, often without food, in cold and exposure. Apart from such external things, there is the daily pressure on me of concern for all the churches. Who is weak without my being weak? Who is led into sin without my intense concern?* (2 Corinthians 11: 23-29).

The worst thing is that some people do not even realize they are lost.

It was costly for Paul in terms of his **family**. Paul never mentioned a family in terms of a personal relationship. Perhaps when Paul gave his life to Christ, he was disinherited by his family and lost all those relationships.

The worst thing is that some people do not even realize they are lost. Many of them are religious and belong to good churches. They give of their finances and have been baptized. Their name is on the church roll but not in the Lamb's Book of Life.

On the one hand, it is hard to let go of our sins; but on the other hand, it is hard to let go of our righteousness and say, "Lord, I don't have anything to offer to you." But Jesus said: *For whoever wishes to save his life will lose it, but whoever loses his life for My sake and the gospel's will save it* (Mark 8:35). That is what Paul meant when he said, "I count all these things but loss. Not only am I willing to turn from my sin, but I am also willing to turn from my righteousness which is in the sight of God as filthy rags." Paul told the Galatians, *If righteousness comes through the Law, then Christ died needlessly* (2:21).

Our Benefits with Christ

- **The Knowledge of Christ**
  Paul wrote, *I count them but rubbish so that I may gain Christ* (Philippians 3:8). The very first thing he gained as new wealth was the knowledge of Christ—not knowledge about Christ but knowledge to know Him and have fellowship with Him.

- **The Fellowship of Christ**
  And may be found in him (Philippians 3:9). That is a safe place to be. It is not that we are just church members but that we are in Christ. We are in His body, and He is in us. We have fellowship with Him—never to be alone again. We can be alone but never lonely because Christ is in us and we are in Christ. Paul exchanged a set of rules for a beloved friend. Before, he had the law; now, he had the Lord!

- **Righteousness Through Christ**
  To be "in Christ" for Paul meant that it was worth more than all of his religion, all of his pharisaism, all of his culture, all of his race, and all of his ritualism. It was Jesus—not only knowledge of Jesus and fellowship with Jesus but also righteousness through Jesus.

Paul was tired of trying to work his way to heaven; legalism was a hard taskmaster, but he was determined to start trusting. *But to the one who does not work, but believes in Him who justifies the ungodly, his faith is credited as righteousness, just as David also speaks of the blessing on the man to whom God credits righteousness apart from works* (Romans 4:5-6). Paul had been doing some accounting of his life.

When we believe in the Lord Jesus Christ—apart from our works, our baptism, our church membership, our trying to keep the Ten Commandments and the Golden Rule—and come to Him and say, "I believe on the Lord Jesus Christ," God makes us righteous at that moment. It is righteousness imputed to us. *Not having a righteousness of my own derived from the Law, but that which is through faith in Christ, the righteousness which comes from God on the basis of faith* (Philippians 3:9).

He is not a prize at the end of the race but a gift so we can run the race.

A housekeeper who worked for a man who was mean and cruel gave her life to Christ. After her salvation, she was exceedingly happy. Her employer despised her happiness in Christ and tried to ridicule and belittle her. Finally, he said to her, "Betty, you say you're saved. Tell me how it feels to be saved." She responded, "Well, I don't believe I can explain it to where you can understand it, but it feels as though I am standing in Jesus's shoes and He is standing in mine." A theologian could not have said it any better.

When we see the bankruptcy of our old nature—not just our sinful nature but also our good nature, we lay it all aside so that we might gain Christ. He is not a prize at the end of the race but a gift so we can run the race.

Salvation is not easy, free, or cheap. Jesus Christ shed His blood and died in agony so that we might have eternal life. On the one hand are our self-righteousness, our legalism, and our trying to be saved while on the other hand is the righteousness of God which is by faith in the Lord Jesus Christ and based on His shed blood. Which will we choose?

Suppose a man owned a 10-acre garbage dump out in the country. Suppose someone approaches him and says, "I've got 10 square miles in New York City that I will exchange for your 10-acre garbage dump." Obviously, that would be an incredible deal, and the man would be crazy not to make the trade.

Paul is telling us to do the math. If we come to the Lord Jesus Christ, He will exchange all of our spiritual garbage that we have been depending on to get us to heaven for the unsearchable riches of Jesus Christ and what He did on the cross.

It is just a matter of doing the math.

If we choose this world and what it has to offer, we have everything to lose and nothing to gain. If we choose Jesus and what He did for us on the cross, we have everything to gain and nothing to lose. It is just a matter of doing the math.

15

THAT I MAY KNOW CHRIST

When Paul was on the Damascus Road and had an encounter with the Lord Jesus Christ, he asked, *Who are You, Lord? The Lord replied, I am Jesus* (Acts 9:5). The day Paul met Jesus, his life was forever changed.

When we meet the Lord Jesus Christ and become personally acquainted with Him, it changes our life forever. *This is eternal life, that they may know You, the only true God, and Jesus Christ whom You have sent* (John 17:3). After Paul met Jesus, he could say, "I know Jesus."

It is possible to know about a person but not really know the person. There is a difference between knowing about Jesus and actually knowing Jesus. We can have a head knowledge without having a heart knowledge, but the heart knowledge does not come without a personal relationship with Jesus. *If you confess with your mouth Jesus as Lord, and believe in your heart that God raised Him from the dead, you will be saved* (Romans 10:9).

When Paul told the Philippians, *That I may know Him* (3:10), we might think, "Wait a minute, Paul. I thought you already knew Jesus. I thought you met Him on the Damascus Road and had a personal experience with Him." Indeed, he did; but when we first meet someone, that is just the beginning. We do not know everything there is to know about an individual at first acquaintance but learn more about them as we go along.

There is a difference between knowing about Jesus and actually knowing Jesus.

For those who are married, when they met their husband or wife, they certainly did not know everything there was to know about them. When we are getting to know someone, there is the beginning experience; but as the relationship grows and develops, we learn more and more about them with many surprises to come along the way.

This is what Paul was talking about. "I want to know Jesus better. I want to know more about Him. I want to know more about what it means to know Him." Philippians 3:10 is one of the greatest passages in the Bible on the subject of knowing Jesus in a personal and powerful way.

OUR RELATIONSHIP TO CHRIST BRINGS POWER INTO OUR LIFE.

That I may know Him and the power of His resurrection (Philippians 3:10). Our relationship with Jesus will bring power into our life.

A Desirable Power

The power of God is desirable and something we need and must have. Mankind has great power in many ways; yet for all of the power we have, we still understand that we are very weak individuals.

The greatest display of power is the resurrection of Jesus.

A man who knows how to operate earth-moving equipment is strong in that way; but when he comes home at night, he cannot control his temper or his tongue or his foul language. He is strong in one way but weak in another. We have the power to put people in a rocket and send them into outer space, but many do not have the power to take a family and grow them to be strong and productive in society.

That I may know Him and the power of His resurrection (Philippians 3:10). We know that we need power because we are weak in and of ourselves. The power of God is desirable.

A Demonstrated Power

The power of His resurrection. When God raised Jesus from the dead, it was the greatest manifestation of the power of God ever demonstrated. As mortal men and women, we do not have that kind of power. We can do many things with our technology and our natural abilities, but we cannot raise people from the dead. However, Christ voluntarily put Himself in the icy grip of death and three days later arose. That is incredible power!

We see the power of God demonstrated in many ways—in creation and in sustaining the universe; but the greatest display of power is the resurrection of Jesus. This power is available to us for Paul said, *That I may know Him and the power of His resurrection*. It is because of the resurrection that we can know Jesus in a personal way.

We cannot come to know dead people. They are already dead, and we cannot have a personal relationship with them. We cannot be introduced to Buddha because he is dead. We cannot be introduced to Muhammad because he is dead. However, we can be introduced to Jesus Christ because two thousand years ago, He rose from the dead and is alive forevermore. His presence is with us. We can have a personal relationship with Christ.

Paul writes about this same kind of power and uses similar terminology: *I pray that the eyes of your heart may be enlightened, so that you will know what is the hope of His calling, what are the riches of the glory of His inheritance in the saints* (Ephesians 1:18).

Knowing Jesus brings pain into our life.

And what is the surpassing greatness of His power toward us who believe. These are in accordance with the working of the strength of His might (Ephesians 1:19). That is the kind of power God says we can know! When we receive Jesus and come to know Him, the power of the resurrected Christ is available in our life.

We can have the power to overcome temptation. Even though we may have the same temptations after receiving Christ as we did before, we now have the power to overcome them. Not only do we have the same temptations as before but also the same problems. We go back to the same job with the same problems we had before we met Jesus. The good news is that there is now the power of the resurrected Jesus available in our life to meet the temptations, to cope with the problems, and to encounter crises and come through victoriously. The power of God is available to us.

There is approximately one tenth of a watt of power in our nervous systems. That is not even enough power to turn on a light bulb. How is it then that we think we can deal with the issues of life in our own strength and ability? *That I may know Him and the power of His resurrection.*

A man trying to survive on one tenth of a watt of power walks into a darkened room and says, "I can't make it. I can't overcome the darkness in this room." On the wall is a switch. If he would just walk over to the switch and flip it, the darkened room would be bathed in light. How foolish to stand and moan about the darkness and our own weaknesses when there is available power in the room and all we have to do is flip the switch.

God has given us a switch. The switch that brings the power of God into our life is our faith in Christ. We must trust Jesus and turn to Him. We should begin every day of our lives by claiming the power of the resurrected Lord and praying, "Dear Jesus, live through me today. I need Your power to face this job that I can't stand. I've got a family problem, and I don't know how to deal with it. I need Your power." The very power that raised Jesus from the dead is available in our life. *That I may know Him* brings power into our life.

OUR RELATIONSHIP WITH CHRIST BRINGS PAIN IN OUR LIFE.

Knowing Jesus brings pain into our life, and we are rarely prepared for this strange truth.

That I may know Him and the power of His resurrection and the fellowship of His sufferings (Philippians 3:10). Jesus was *a man of sorrows* (Isaiah 53:3). The Hebrew word should literally be translated a "man of pains."

Social Pain

Jesus experienced social pain, specifically in his hometown. He was talked about and made fun of. At the height of His ministry, His family *went out to take custody of Him; for they were saying, "He has lost His senses"* (Mark 3:21).

Emotional Pain

Jesus experienced emotional pain because the people called him illegitimate, blasphemous, and possessed by Beelzebul.

Physical Pain

Jesus experienced physical pain. Though His body was not tainted by human sin, its sensitivities were at the highest degree. Consider the pain of the crown of thorns, the nails in His hands and feet, the spear in His side. He knew physical pain like no one else has ever experienced.

Spiritual Pain

Jesus experienced spiritual pain. The worst pain that will ever be known is a soul that dies and goes to hell. On the cross, Jesus endured the pains of hell.

That I may know Him . . . and the fellowship of His sufferings (Philippians 3:10). What is meant by sharing in the pain of Jesus's sufferings?

Now I rejoice in my sufferings for your sake, and in my flesh I do my share on behalf of His body, which is the church, in filling up what is lacking in Christ's afflictions (Colossians 1:24). Paul said, "I want to fill up that which is behind the afflictions of the sufferings of Christ."

But to the degree that you share the sufferings of Christ, keep on rejoicing, so that also at the revelation of His glory you may rejoice with exultation (1 Peter 4:13). Peter declared that believers partake in the sufferings and pains of Christ. As Christians, we experience the same kinds of things Jesus experienced on this earth.

But He was pierced through for our transgressions . . . that was His pain . . . *He was crushed for our iniquities . . .* that was His pain . . . *the chastening for our well-being fell upon Him . . .* that was His pain . . . *and by His scourging we are healed . . .* that was His pain (Isaiah 53:5). We cannot enter into those kinds of pains; He suffered in order that souls might be saved.

There is something about the Christian life that brings pain into our existence because of our relationship with Jesus. It is like when we fall in love with someone and they become our mate. We love them dearly; and from that point on, whatever pain they endure, we endure. If the wife gets sick and hurts, the husband hurts. If the husband suffers, the wife suffers. When we love someone, we enter into their pain.

It is often the painful experiences in life that draw us closer to Jesus.

When we go to the dentist, we want our gums numbed because we do not want to feel the pain. We will do most anything to kill the pain; however, it is often the painful experiences in life that draw us closer to Jesus and teach us more of who Jesus is and what He can do in our life.

OUR RELATIONSHIP WITH CHRIST BRINGS PURPOSE INTO OUR LIFE.

For many people, life has no purpose. They are merely living their existence, and it is totally meaningless. They have no sense of direction, no goal or motivation in life. That is why they often turn to things such as drugs and alcohol. They look for all kinds of amusements and wrap themselves in material things because life holds no meaning; but when they come to know Christ as Savior, He gives them a purpose in life.

Our Immediate Purpose

God's immediate purpose for our life is *being conformed to His death* (Philippians 3:10). Jesus said if we would give our life to Him and come to know Him, He would give us purpose. Visions of romance and adventure fill our minds. "That's wonderful

Lord. You've got a plan for my life. I can't wait to find out what it's going to be." Jesus says, "I want you to die." We respond, "Lord, that's not exactly what I had in mind." However, Paul said: *That I may know Him and the power of His resurrection and the fellowship of His sufferings, being conformed to His death.* God says, "My immediate purpose for your life is that you may die."

We cannot have a resurrection until there has been a crucifixion.

There are two crosses in the New Testament—the cross of our Savior and our own cross. Jesus said, *If anyone wishes to come after Me, he must deny himself, and take up his cross and follow Me* (Mark 8:34). Paul said, *I have been crucified with Christ* (Galatians 2:20).

Crucifixion is not something a person can do to themselves. They can drive nails into their feet and one hand but not on the other hand. That means that every day of our life, we must come to the Lord and say, "Lord, let's have a funeral this morning." Paul said, *I die daily* (1 Corinthians 15:31).

The immediate purpose for our life is that every day, we die to our own desires and our own plans. That is the only way to be useful in life, the only way to be helpful, the only way to find fulfillment. We cannot have a resurrection until there has been a crucifixion.

Our Ultimate Purpose

God's ultimate purpose for our life: *If by any means I might attain unto the resurrection of the dead* (Philippians 3:11 KJV). Paul was not expressing doubt but a spirit of humility with the use of the phrase, *if by any means.* He was saying, "I don't deserve it." This passage literally means to experience resurrection from among the dead. God is saying, "If you come to know Jesus as your personal Savior, one day I will raise you from the dead."

We may die physically, but there will be a resurrection. God will take us out of the grave and deliver us. We will be caught up to meet the Lord in the air to be eternally with Christ. *Then I will know fully just as I also have been fully known* (1 Corinthians 13:12), and forever we will get to know more and more of the Lord Jesus Christ.

From among the dead, there is going to be another resurrection. *All who are in the tombs will hear His voice, and will come forth; those who did the good deeds to a resurrection of life, those who committed the evil deeds to a resurrection of judgment* (John 5:28-29). A resurrection unto life and the resurrection of condemnation.

I met Jesus on a Sunday morning when I was 12 years of age. A new person came into my life, someone I had never known before. I had known about Him; but that morning, I came to know Him in a personal way.

When we meet some people, it seems that the more we get to know them, the less we like them, the more inconsistent they seem to be, and the more we realize all their faults and failings. However, the day anyone meets Jesus, from that day on, the more they know about Him, the more they love Him, and the more they can truly sing, "Every day with Jesus is sweeter than the day before. Every day with Jesus, I love Him more and more."

16

WINNING THE CHRISTIAN RACE

As we read the letters of the Apostle Paul, it becomes very apparent that he was familiar with athletic activities as he uses all types of athletic terminology. Perhaps on his missionary journeys to the various major cities of the ancient world, he would stop by stadiums and attend games and, in doing so, would draw many analogies and lessons about life. Paul came to see that the Christian life was very much like a race.

In the New Testament era, the Olympic Games included track and field events—the main event being running. Paul described the Christian life like a race—a race to become what God wants us to be. In that context, it helps us understand what seems to be a contradiction between Philippians 3:12 and 3:15.

Verse 12 states, *Not that I have already obtained it or have already become perfect.* Verse 15 states, *Let us therefore, as many as are perfect.* We must note that Paul was not talking about sinless perfection. The contextual idea is not our being perfect in the terms of being sinless; rather, he was writing about maturity, our progress in the Christian life, and talking about relative perfection, not ultimate perfection.

An example would be a child growing up and going through the various stages of development. At age 12 we would say of her, "She is a perfect 12-year-old." That does not mean she is a grown woman but in that stage in her development, she is a perfect 12-year-old girl.

Paul was not talking about sinless perfection.

Consider a man who is running the mile. He clocks off the first lap of the four laps. Those timing him say he had a perfect first lap. That does not mean the race is over or that he might not improve and make additional progress. It means that at that stage in the race, he is exactly where he needs to be which is what Paul was saying. We are in a race. We are in the race of the Christian life, a race toward maturity.

We must be ready to start the race; it begins today. We are at the starting line, the gun fires, and the race begins. We are to follow the progress of the Christian race.

FINDING CHRIST IN THE RACE.

Not as though I had already attained, either were already perfect: but I follow after, if that I may apprehend that for which also I am apprehended of Christ Jesus (Philippians 3:12 KJV). Paul was talking about the start of the race.

Apprehend

The word "apprehended" means to lay hold of. Paul was talking about his experience of salvation—when the race began in his life. This may sound trite, but it is absolutely essential: We cannot run the race until we begin the race. There must be a time when we get in position on the starting block to be ready when the gun fires to start the race. Paul's race began on the Damascus Road when the Lord Jesus Christ "apprehended" him or laid hold of him and his life.

***Jesus lays hold of us in grace,
and we lay hold of Him by faith.***

The same thing is true for every believer. If we have truly been saved and know Christ as our Savior, there was a time when Jesus laid hold of our life. It might have been in a church service or while watching television or at our bedside. Jesus apprehended us and laid hold of our life. *Take hold of the eternal life to which you were called* (1 Timothy 6:12). Jesus lays hold of us in grace, and we lay hold of Him by faith.

That I may apprehend that . . . The gun has been fired. The Christian life has begun.

Apprehensive

Paul then says, *I am apprehended of Christ Jesus*. He has not yet arrived; he has not yet attained. He is apprehensive. "I have not yet become everything Jesus has saved me to become."

A first grader went to school on the first day of school and came home on Friday and announced to his mom, "I'm not going back to school next week." She asked, "Why not?" He said, "Because they can't teach me any more."

Sometimes Christians think that way. They believe they have arrived in the Christian life, but we never arrive in the Christian life. We do not know everything there is to know about the Bible. We have not grown the way God wants us to grow in the Christian life so we make up our mind that we have not yet arrived, that we have not yet apprehended, that we are not yet everything God wants us to be.

Alfred, Lord Tennyson was one of the greatest poets of all time. His poem, "In Memoriam," is one of the greatest ever written, and he spent 17 years writing it and would likely have rewritten portions of the poem numerous times. He never arrived; he never reached perfection.

We must remember that there is a race yet to be run.

FOLLOWING CHRIST IN THE RACE.

Perhaps we are an athlete. Perhaps we are a runner or a jogger. Paul uses a picture of running the race and how it applies to making progress in the Christian life. The gun has been fired. The race has begun. We are now running the race.

Concentration on the Present

Paul gave us several crucial elements of running the race. *I do not regard myself as having laid hold of it yet; but* **one thing** *I do* (Philippians 3:13, Emphasis added). Paul was concentrating on the present.

The Bible uses the phrase **one thing** numerous times:

- The blind man said of Jesus when He healed him, *Whether He is a sinner, I do not know;* **one thing** *I do know, that though I was blind, now I see* (John 9:25, Emphasis added).
- **One thing** *I have asked from the Lord, that I shall seek: That I may dwell in the house of the Lord all the days of my life, To behold the beauty of the Lord And to meditate in His temple* (Psalm 27:4, Emphasis added).
- Looking at the rich young ruler, *Jesus felt a love for him and said to him, "***One thing*** you lack: go and sell all you possess and give to the poor, and you will have treasure in heaven; and come, follow Me"* (Mark 10:21, Emphasis added).

- Jesus said to Martha, *Only **one thing** is necessary, for Mary has chosen the good part, which shall not be taken away from her* (Luke 10:42, Emphasis added).

Paul picked up the terminology of *one thing* and said that he was putting total concentration on the race—a concentration on the present.

We are not a wandering generality but a definite specific!

There is tremendous power in concentration. One of the things that makes an electric drill so powerful is the tremendous concentration of power at one point. Consider the concentration of a great concert pianist or a field goal specialist on a football team. Both concentrate their efforts and work tirelessly on doing that one thing.

Paul told us we need to concentrate our total attention on the assignment of running the race for the Lord Jesus Christ. We are not a wandering generality but a definite specific! There are too many Christians who do not say, *But one thing I do*, but say instead, "These 40 things I dabble in." *Teach me Your way, O Lord; I will walk in Your truth; Unite my heart to fear Your name* (Psalm 86:11).

As Christians, are we focused? Are we in a zone about our Christian life? How is it that Christians think they can grow and mature in their Christian life and not have total concentration? We cannot read the Bible sporadically, attend church spasmodically, and pray occasionally and expect to be successful in the Christian life. We must concentrate on the present and be able to say, *But one thing I do*.

If we want to be a victorious Christian who excels, then we must be like the runner: *But one thing I do*. We must get our mind on what we are doing.

Obliteration of the Past

We must also forget *what lies behind* (Philippians 3:13). There must be an obliteration of the past.

God said, *I will forgive their iniquity, and their sin I will remember no more* (Jeremiah 31:34); and *I WILL BE MERCIFUL TO THEIR INIQUITIES, AND I WILL REMEMBER THEIR SINS NO MORE* (Hebrews 8:12). These verses do not mean that God has some kind of divine amnesia and does not remember our sin.

The load of tomorrow added to that of yesterday and carried today makes the strongest falter.

Paul was not saying that we will not have any memories of the past but that we are not to allow the past to influence or affect us. We are not to let the past keep us from winning the race. We are not to run looking back over our shoulder. Runners who have competed in races know that one of the basic rules of winning the race is never to look back over their shoulder.

Some Christians never make progress in the Christian life because they are dwelling on the past. It has been said that memory is a nursery where children, now grown old, play with broken toys. The load of tomorrow added to that of yesterday and carried today makes the strongest falter.

One of the things that we should forget is our past sins. If we have confessed them to God, He has forgiven us. We must accept God's forgiveness because our sins are buried in the *depths of the sea* (Micah 7:19).

One of the things we should forget is our past failures. There is no need to cry over spilled milk. All have failed. Thomas Edison, the great inventor, conducted thousands of experiments that failed before he invented the electric light bulb. We must build on our mistakes, not dwell them.

One of the things we should forget is our past successes. It is so easy for a church to dwell on the past and say, "We used to do this way," or "We used to do it that way," or "I liked it the way it used to be." The past is gone forever. While we thank God for the successes and blessings of the past, we are living in the present.

One of the things we should forget is our past grievances. "They did me wrong, and I was counting on them." Many Christians have past grievances that eat their hearts out, wreck their Christian life, and spoil their testimony. They become bitter, grumpy, complaining believers because they dwell on past grievances. Joseph had an opportunity to be like that with his own brothers; but he said instead, *You meant evil against me, but God meant it for good* (Genesis 50:20). God is in charge and knows what He is doing in our life.

Pressing Toward the Mark

The runner is on the move: *But one thing I do*—concentration on the present; *forgetting what lies behind*—obliteration of the past; *reaching forward to what lies ahead*—total concentration on the future.

Every muscle in the runner's body is stretching and straining. His heart is pumping blood furiously. His lungs are taking in great chunks of oxygen. His feet are pounding the surface of the track. He is totally stretched out—reaching toward those things that are before him.

Paul was teaching us how to live the Christian life—looking toward the future. We should live the Christian life thinking about what we can do for Jesus Christ tomorrow and about what God is going to do in our life today. It is not the time to give up in the race. It is time to keep on stretching all the way to the finish line.

FINISHING FOR CHRIST IN THE RACE.

The first picture is starting the race. The second picture is running the race. The third picture is winning the race.

I press on toward the goal for the prize (Philippians 3:14). Paul was talking about winning the race—the mark to be reached. He was in the home stretch and saw the tape of the finish line ahead.

The Mark to Reach

Fixing our eyes on Jesus, the author and perfecter of faith (Hebrews 12:2). Jesus starts us in the race and is the finisher of our faith. Jesus is at the starting line to get us going and at the finish line to welcome us when we get there. The goal of the race is to be like Jesus. The purpose of the Christian life is to be like Jesus Christ.

I press on toward the goal for the prize of the upward call of God in Christ Jesus (Philippians 3:14). Paul is running now towards the tape.

The Medal to Reward

When the runner turns the last curve and heads into the final stretch and hits the tape, he knows it is time for the reward. There is thunderous applause from the people in the stands. In Paul's time, an official would come to the runner and say, "You've been called up." The successful, victorious athlete would go to the Emperor's box; and the Emperor would congratulate the successful runner and award him the prize—the emblems of his victory.

An Olympic victor who was a citizen of Athens in the year 600 BC could expect to receive a cash award of 500 drachmai, a literal fortune. From an Athenian inscription of the 5th century BC, Olympic victors received a free meal in the City Hall every day for the rest of their lives, a kind of early pension plan. Later, in the Hellenistic and Roman periods, pensions for athletes became more formalized and could actually be bought and sold.

WINNING THE CHRISTIAN RACE

Do you not know that those who run in a race all run, but only one receives the prize? Run in such a way that you may win (1 Corinthians 9:24). In a race, one person wins the prize; but as Christians, everyone can win the prize. Someday we will all "hit the tape," and the Lord will say, *there is laid up for me the crown of righteousness, which the Lord, the righteous Judge, will award to me on that day* (2 Timothy 4:8). God will give each of us a medal, and perhaps it will be engraved with "Well done" for *Well done, good and faithful servant* (Matthew 25:23 NIV).

The goal of the race is to be like Jesus.

In 2 Timothy, the last book of which we have any record that Paul wrote, he said, *I have fought the good fight, I have finished the course, I have kept the faith; in the future there is laid up for me the crown of righteousness, which the Lord, the righteous Judge, will award to me on that day; and not only to me, but also to all who have loved His appearing* (2 Timothy 4:7-8).

There came a day that the Roman guards of the Mamertime Prison took Paul across the highway to the guillotine and placed his head on the chopping block. The blade came down, severing his head from his body; and his head rolled into the dust. Someone may have said, "Poor Paul. He just bit the dust." However, that was not the case. Paul "hit the tape"; and Jesus said, "Well done Paul. You've run a good race. Here's your prize."

There are those who die unknown and unmourned on obscure mission fields, and some may think, "That poor missionary bit the dust." No, that missionary "hit the tape."

Not far from the Matterhorn in Switzerland is a cemetery where many of the great mountain climbers are buried. On one of the tombstones is written, "He died climbing." What an epitaph!

"Lord, lift me up and let me stand, By faith, on heaven's tableland, A higher plane than I have found; Lord, plant my feet on higher ground" (Higher Ground, Johnson Oatman, Jr., 1898).

17

THE HEAVENLY-MINDED LEADER

How we view ourselves in this life often shapes our views and values. In Philippians 3, we find three pictures of the Christian life:

- The first metaphor Paul uses is of an accountant: *I count it all* (3:8 KJV).
- The second metaphor is of a runner: *I press on* (3:14).
- The third metaphor is of a traveler or a pilgrim: *We eagerly wait for a Savior* (3:20).

The Christian life is like an accountant, an athlete, and an alien. We are just passing through this world on our way to our eternal home.

Brethren, join in following my example, and observe those who walk according to the pattern you have in us. For many walk, of whom I often told you, and now tell you even weeping, that they are enemies of the cross of Christ, whose end is destruction, whose god is their appetite, and whose glory is in their shame, who set their minds on earthly things. For our citizenship is in heaven, from which also we eagerly wait for a Savior, the Lord Jesus Christ; who will transform the body of our humble state into conformity with the body of His glory, by the exertion of the power that He has even to subject all things to Himself (Philippians 3:17-21).

Jesus used the picture of life as a journey saying that there are two ways to travel—*enter through the narrow gate; for the gate is wide and the way is broad that leads to destruction* (Matthew 7:13).

Every one of us is on a journey with a destination in sight.

Unfortunately, many *set their minds on earthly things* (Philippians 3:19) rather than on heavenly things. One entails an earthly path while the other entails a heavenly path. Every one of us is on a journey with a destination in sight. We are either placing our priorities and affections on earthly things, or we have our eyes and affections set on heavenly things.

MANAGING EARTHLY THINGS

Observe those who walk according to the pattern you have in us. For many walk, of whom I often told you, and now tell you even weeping, that they are enemies of the cross of Christ (Philippians 3:17-18). Paul is speaking of those who have made the earth their total focus in life and are living for the present. We live in a generation that is fast becoming earth-bound pagans, people who live with only this world in view and who have put their mind only on what they can see and profit from.

Not everyone whose name is on the church roll is also on heaven's roll.

Picture Paul in the Roman prison cell with tears running down his cheeks as he writes to the church at Philippi. Perhaps one of the soldiers guarding him says, "I don't blame you, Paul. If I were in prison, I'd be weeping too." Paul responds, "I'm not crying for myself," to which the soldier says, "I understand; I'm sure you're weeping for your family and hate to be separated from them." Paul counters, "I'm not weeping for my family." Again, the soldier says, "I understand. You are surely weeping because of what your enemies have done to you"; but Paul exclaims, "Yes, I am weeping for my enemies, but I am not weeping because of what they've done to me. I am weeping for the enemies of the cross."

We sometimes get the idea that everyone in the New Testament church was saved and tend to idealize these individuals and believers. However, 1 John 2:19 tells us that *they went out from us, but they were not really of us; for if they had been of us, they would have remained with us; but they went out, so that it would be shown that they all are not of us.*

Not everyone whose name is on the church roll is also on heaven's roll. Each person must truly be born again and have Christ as their Savior. Following are three descriptions Paul gave of those who are earthly-minded.

Every Life Has a Destiny

In speaking of those who are enemies of the cross of Christ, Paul emphatically wrote that their *end is destruction* (Philippians

3:19). Every life has a destiny, every life has a goal, and every life has an end. Their *end is destruction* which reveals a wasted life.

A terrible picture is painted of those who do not know Christ as their Savior. Many are so concerned about the political right and the political left when they need to be concerned about the above (heaven) and the below (hell). When we die, it will not matter whether we are a conservative or a liberal or a Republican or a Democrat. The bottom line is whether we are saved or lost. Some may not care for what is termed "scare tactics"; however, there is nothing wrong with fear as a motive.

Many people today give no thought or concern to their sin.

A traffic officer pulled a person over and said, "If you don't slow down this car, you are going to have a wreck and kill yourself." A scare tactic but true.

A person went to the doctor who told them, "If you don't lose 40 pounds, it is going to seriously affect your health." Hopefully, it alarmed the person enough that they got serious about losing the weight. Fear is not a bad motive. It has been said that "I'd rather scare you into heaven than lull you into hell."

Every Life Has a Deity

In speaking of those who are enemies of the cross of Christ, Paul also wrote that their *god is their appetite* (Philippians 3:19). Paul told them they indeed had a deity, and their god was their "belly." He used the same phrase again in Romans 16:18: *For such men are slaves, not of our Lord Christ but of their own appetites; and by their smooth and flattering speech they deceive the hearts of the unsuspecting.*

Paul spoke not only about physical appetites but also about living for the physical pleasures of life which include food, drugs, and all of the things that are pleasurable yet unhealthy in life. Paul told them those things had become their gods.

Many people live with no eternal perspective. They have no heavenly vantage point and are merely living for the things of this earth and trying to make it through the week to get to the party on the weekend. They are interested in rougher parties, faster cars, more elaborate houses, and looser sex. They are living only for the physical pleasures of life. Their *god is their appetite.*

However, there is more to life than the physical. We not only have a belly but also a soul, and the things of this world will not satisfy the human soul. God has made the soul so that it can only be satisfied through a relationship with Him. We can try all of the pleasures of life and travel all the roads of the material things that this life has to offer, and it is all a dead-end street. We will only find joy, satisfaction, and genuine pleasure in life when we develop a relationship with the Lord Jesus Christ.

Every Life Has a Depravity

Paul did not mince words when he said *that they are enemies of the cross of Christ . . . whose glory is in their shame* (Philippians 3:18-19). Those who sell out to material and physical pleasures and live only from an earthly perspective eventually arrive at the point where their spiritual sensitivities are so dull that they glory and brag about the things of which they should be ashamed.

This is a picture of the world in which we live—the drunkenness in our nation that people brag about and the immorality portrayed in our movies, music, and television programs. There was a time when people blushed when they were embarrassed. Now it seems they are embarrassed if they blush. Their *glory is in their shame*—a picture of what life is if lived only from an earthly perspective.

A man returning from a business trip noticed a huge fire with smoke billowing into the sky as the plane he was on was preparing to land. He said, "Would you look at that! What a fire!" Without giving it another thought, he got into his car after disembarking and began the drive to his office. The closer he got, the more he became aware that the flames and smoke were coming from his own business. That to which he had given no thought or concern was destroying his own livelihood.

Many people today give no thought or concern to their sin. They ignore immorality and glory in the things that ought to cause shame—the very things that are destroying and wrecking their life.

There are untold numbers of people who are minding earthly things and, according to Paul, are enemies of the cross of Christ. An immoral life on the part of one who claims to be a Christian is a life that is in total contradiction to everything the cross of Jesus Christ intended. Jesus did not die that we could live any way we choose. Jesus did not die so that we could live immoral and impure lives. Jesus died on the cross to give us power to live clean, pure, godly, and dedicated lives.

MINDING HEAVENLY THINGS

For our citizenship is in heaven, from which also we eagerly wait for a Savior, the Lord Jesus Christ (Philippians 3:20). Paul was talking about those who manage heavenly things, those who have come to understand that this world is not the only world but that there is a better one ahead.

Our Heavenly Citizenship

That Paul was a Roman citizen was significant but even more so in the city of Philippi for Philippi was a Roman colony that was governed by Roman law. They wore Roman clothing and tried to emulate the life of Rome. Rome had also settled a number of retired soldiers there.

Consequently, when Paul said, *our citizenship is in heaven*, they immediately understood that he was saying that we have a citizenship beyond this world. We have a heavenly homeland.

Jesus said, *You must be born again* (John 3:7). The word *again* can be translated "from above." *You must be born* from above.

Every person who is saved has a heavenly homeland—a homeland with walls of jasper, gates of pearl, and streets of gold. A homeland that has no jails, no prisons, and no funeral homes. A homeland that has no hospitals and no asylums. A homeland that has no fighting, no war, no sorrow, no pain, no heartache, and no death.

We should live in such a way that people get a little glimpse of heaven.

We are moving toward heaven. We are not to go around with some kind of mystical look on our face or a far-off look in our eye or talking like we have a steeple in our throat. We take on heavenly standards and heaven's viewpoint and bring that to bear on our daily life.

Once we are born again, we no longer belong down here. Since our homeland is in heaven, we apply heavenly standards to our decisions and lifestyle every day of our life. We do our business with our homeland in mind. We do our schoolwork with heaven in mind. We interact with our family with eternity in mind. We live with the awareness that our homeland is in heaven and we are to live as heavenly citizens down here.

Jesus was what might be called "the heavenly man" for He said, *I am from above* (John 8:23). Everywhere Jesus went, He brought a little fragrance of heaven to life. That is the way it should be with us. We should live in such a way that people get a little glimpse of heaven. Our behavior and our lifestyle should be such that people are aware that our citizenship is in heaven.

Our Heavenly Anticipation

For our conversation is in heaven; from whence also we look for the Saviour, the Lord Jesus Christ (Philippians 3:20 KJV). The word *look* is a combination of words put together that means to look away to. It is the idea of tiptoe expectancy. The Bible teaches us that while we are living in this world, we are aware that we do not belong to this world. Additionally, we look with anticipation for Jesus to come back to this world to take us with Him.

We should live every day of our life as if Jesus were coming today.

In those days, the greatest event that could ever happen in the life of a city would be for Caesar to visit. The announcement would be made that "Caesar is coming!" and they would clean the houses, wash the streets, and repair the roads. The city would be filled with intense desire and anticipation. All of the citizens would be looking forward to the emperor's coming to their city.

We have someone who is coming for us, and His name is Jesus. We are to live *looking for the blessed hope and the appearing of the glory of our great God and Savior, Christ Jesus* (Titus 2:13).

A man once visited a magnificent villa that had a beautiful garden. Talking to the man who tended that garden, the man said, "Sir, you are tending this garden as if your master would come tomorrow." The gardener replied, "As if he would come today, Sir."

We should live every day of our life as if Jesus were coming today. It would change our life and our behavior. It would affect the decisions we make.

Our Heavenly Transformation

Who will transform the body of our humble state (Philippians 3:21). Paul is referring to the frailty and failures of our human body. Every day of our life we come to understand more and more how frail our body is—our body with all of its burdens, frustrations, limitations, and humiliations. Soon and very soon, however, we are going to experience a glorious transformation and have a body like the resurrected, ascended, glorified body of Jesus Christ. In His glorified body, Jesus could appear and disappear. He was not restricted by time or matter or space.

No doubt we all have loved ones we have placed in a casket, and their body was one of humiliation and a body of decay. However, that is not the end. One of these days, there will be a glorious resurrection day. We should live every day of our life in anticipation of the time when He will transform our body.

Paul was talking with Agrippa about the resurrection and said, *Why is it considered incredible among you people if God does raise the dead?* (Acts 26:8). He was saying, "Why is it incredible to believe that God can cause us to live again when He has caused us to live in the first place?" When we think of the miracle of life, we must consider all of the combinations of cells in the human body and the fact that God breathed the breath of life into that body.

Some say that life came into existence by intelligent design. Indeed, it did; and the name of the intelligent designer was the Lord God of the universe. The same God who created us and gave us life in the first place will one day give us life eternal *by the exertion of the power that He has even to subject all things to Himself* (Philippians 3:21).

God *is able also to save forever those who draw near to God through Him* (Hebrews 7:25).

God *is able to come to the aid of those who are tempted* (Hebrews 2:18).

God *is able to do far more abundantly beyond all that we ask or think, according to the power that works within us* (Ephesians 3:20).

There is nothing God cannot do. God can save our life, give us joy, and cause us to be happy. God can give us victory over temptations that are plaguing us and are like a chain around our life.

We must live every day as those who are pilgrims traveling through earth on our way to our heavenly home. We must pick our road and our destination. We can manage earthly things or we can mind heavenly things.

THE PEACE OF THE CHRISTIAN LIFE (PHILIPPIANS 4:1-9)

18

HOW TO HEAL A CHURCH FIGHT

The Book of Philippians is a love letter written by the Apostle Paul, the pastor, to this beloved congregation of believers at the church in Philippi. He stated at the very beginning of his letter that *I thank my God in all my remembrance of you always offering prayer with joy in my every prayer for you all* (Philippians 1:3-4).

Mary then took a pound of very costly perfume of pure nard, and anointed the feet of Jesus and wiped His feet with her hair; and the house was filled with the fragrance of the perfume (John 12:3). Just as the house was filled with the fragrance of the perfume when Mary anointed the feet of Jesus, so there is a fragrance of love between Paul and the church at Philippi because every time he thought about the church, his heart was filled with joy.

There needs to be a fragrance of perfume in the church today. The unity, harmony, ministry, and testimony of a church should send forth a pleasant fragrance.

The Apostle Paul had been writing his heartfelt letter to the believers in Philippi, and we now see one of the reasons for his letter. There was a relationship problem that was affecting the testimony and the ministry of the church.

> *Therefore, my beloved brethren whom I long to see, my joy and crown, in this way stand firm in the Lord, my beloved. I urge Euodia and I urge Syntyche to live in harmony in the Lord. Indeed, true companion, I ask you also to help these women who have shared my struggle in the cause of the gospel, together with Clement also and the rest of my fellow workers, whose names are in the book of life* (Philippians 4:1-3).

All churches have problems because they are made up of people. A church is not a trophy case for the display of perfect believers but a hospital for the recovery and care of born-again believers. However, just because we are saved and are going to heaven when we die does not mean we have lost our sin nature. There are no perfect churches on this earth, and the Philippian church was not perfect either because there was a small problem brewing between two women. At first glance, it may not have seemed to be a major problem; but small problems can often morph into larger problems and cause much damage. Paul addressed this relationship problem and thereby now teaches us to how to handle such issues.

AN APPEAL TO THE ENRICHED PEOPLE

In Philippians 4:1-3, we see firsthand the logical, understandable order as Paul made several appeals. Even though he was appealing to the people in the congregation, we can sense the fragrance of love in the atmosphere.

Cultivate a Christian Atmosphere Through Community

Paul addressed the believers at Philippi as *my beloved brethren*. Many years ago, we also addressed fellow believers as "Brother" and "Sister"; and although there were times when people used this terminology in a trite and casual manner, Paul never did. He started out as an antagonist of the Christian faith, trying to wipe Christianity from the face of the earth. He definitely had no problem killing "brothers and sisters" in Christ. However, after he was saved, Ananias came to him and called him *Brother Saul* (Acts 22:13). It must have broken Paul's heart to hear himself called *Brother*, but he who had been their enemy was now their brother.

A church is not a trophy case for the display of perfect believers but a hospital for the recovery and care of born-again believers.

The words, brother and sister, mean we are in the same family—brothers and sisters in the Lord. It is a moving word that we use in the church and one that should never be used casually.

Cultivate a Christian Atmosphere Through Compassion

In Philippians 4:1, Paul used the words, *my beloved brethren* and *my beloved*. He was telling them that he loved them. He also used the phrase, *whom I long to see*, meaning, "I dearly love you people and am running after you with my love and reaching out to you in my love." How sweet it is when there is love in a fellowship. Love in the body of Christ is special and holds great meaning.

Cultivate a Christian Atmosphere Through Celebration

Paul wrote, *my joy and crown*. He had led many of these people to faith in Christ so when he used that term, he was talking about these believers. Imagine how Paul may have pictured the different individuals in the church in his mind's eye. He could almost feel the warm handshake of Sister Lydia and the bear hug of the burly jailer he had won to Christ. He called them *my joy and crown*.

We are living in a time when God's people must take their stand.

When we lead people to faith in the Lord Jesus Christ, they become a source of joy in our life. The longer we live, the more we understand that one of the greatest sources of joy as a Christian is having had a part in leading people to faith in the Lord Jesus.

Using the expression, *my joy and crown*, he was saying that in the present, they were his joy; but in the future, they would be his crown. On earth, they were a source of rejoicing and in heaven they would be a source of reward. In Paul's mind, earth receded and heaven opened and he saw himself before the Judgment Seat of Christ. As the Lord was handing out the crowns of rejoicing for people who had faith in Christ, one of the crowns which would come to Paul would be engraved: "Philippi."

The question is: Will we have any crowns in heaven for soul-winning—people we have led to the Lord? Imagine how wonderful it would be to have people come up to us and say, "Thank You. It's because of you that I'm in heaven. It's because of you that I came to know Jesus as my Lord and Savior."

Commit to a Christian Advance

Paul said, *Stand firm in the Lord, my beloved* (Philippians 4:1). It was an appeal not only to stand firm but also to keep on standing—a command given to a soldier to stand his ground against the onslaught of the enemy.

We are living in a time when God's people must take their stand. While many are abandoning the field of battle and not standing up for the Lord Jesus Christ, Paul's call was to *stand firm in the Lord*. When others are running, we are to stand firm. When problems are mounting, we are to stand firm. When the going gets tough, we are to stand firm. How? Not in our strength but in the strength of the Lord.

When the going gets tough, we are to stand firm.

Therefore as you have received Christ Jesus the Lord, so walk in Him, having been firmly rooted and now being built up in Him and established in your faith, just as you were instructed (Colossians 2:6-7). We must be firmly rooted and grounded in Christ Jesus just like an oak tree which stands firm when the winds beat against it. Why? Not because of the oak tree's hold on the soil but because of the soil's hold on the oak tree. If we are firmly rooted, we can stand firm when the winds of adversity blow and the enemies of our culture attack our faith.

AN ADDRESS TO AN ESTRANGEMENT PROBLEM

Paul appeals to the problem which had been hinted at gently when he said to *have this attitude in yourselves which was also in Christ Jesus* (Philippians 2:5). He talked about unity and the importance of harmony in the fellowship, but Paul then met the issue head-on and addressed the problem directly by speaking concerning two ladies in the church: *I urge Euodia and I urge Syntyche to live in harmony in the Lord* (Philippians 4:2). Euodia means a prosperous journey and Syntyche fortunate. The word *urge* means to advocate, solicit, or entreat. There was a serious problem developing in the church; and the Apostle Paul, rather than being dictatorial, became very pastoral.

When these two sisters in the Lord got together, the arguments would begin. However, we must remember that Paul said they *have shared my struggle in the cause of the gospel* and their *names are in the book of life* (Philippians 4:3). These were two good women who had had a falling-out.

We must first thank God for the women of the Church and what they have contributed throughout the ages—the sons and daughters they have trained for ministry, the service they have rendered in places where their names were never mentioned, the songs they have written, the supplications and prayers they have offered up to the Lord, and so much more.

Not only is it possible for sisters in the Lord to have problems with one another but also for brothers in the Lord to have problems with one another. It is even possible for deacons to quarrel, choir members to squabble, and young people to argue with one another.

We do not know exactly what happened in Philippi or what the problem specifically was since Paul did not go into detail as to who was right or who was wrong. Perhaps the argument escalated from something small followed by a hateful word which was followed by another until it was a full-blown argument to the point where Euodia and Syntyche were no longer speaking to one another.

Perhaps their spouses became involved and began to enlist sympathizers. Then the church members began to choose sides. It became like a dead fly in the perfume which caused the whole thing to have an odor and quickly reached the point to where Paul had to deal with it.

Consider a possible scenario. The news was out: "Paul has written us a letter!" The next Sunday, the church was jam-packed. They were all there to hear Paul's letter read. All of a sudden like a bolt out of the blue, a clap of thunder, or a crack of lightning, Paul said, *I urge Euodia and I urge Syntyche to live in harmony in the Lord* (Philippians 4:2). He had called out their names! When he said, *Euodia*, she nearly swallowed her tongue. When he said, *Syntyche*, she burst into tears. Imagine the electricity in the church when these sisters were called by name.

It matters not whether we are right.

The time could come when we have to call out names directly and also consider whether Paul could have called out our name. Is there a squabble going on between us and another believer in the fellowship? Is there someone we will not even speak to at church or in the choir or in the youth group? Is there someone we shun and weave our way around?

Picture heaven when the Angel Gabriel or the Apostle Paul introduces folks and says, "I want to introduce Euodia and Syntyche." The new arrival says, "Euodia and Syntyche? The two ladies who had the fuss that Paul mentioned in the Bible?" How embarrassing it would be to be introduced in heaven for having an argument with another believer.

I urge Euodia and I urge Syntyche to live in harmony in the Lord. Though that does not mean they always had to agree on every point, Paul was telling us to settle our differences. Though we do not have to agree on dress or diet or football teams or things of the like, it does mean that we all must agree that the most important thing in a church is to win people to faith in the Lord Jesus Christ and to make certain that nothing is done to harm the unity, harmony, ministry, and testimony of the church. It matters not whether we are right. There are times when we need to be silent before the Lord and let God work out the problem.

AN APPEAL TO AN EXCELLENT PEACEMAKER

Notice the words, *true companion*, that Paul chose in Philippians 4:3. Some believe that the Greek word used means someone who works well in harmony and is a reference to a proper name. Others believe it is a reference to Epaphroditus, the man who brought the letter back. The truth is that we do not really know who it was, but it was someone in the church who was uniquely gifted in being a peacemaker.

Sometimes the fire will fall on the one trying to help others.

Jesus said, *Blessed are the peacemakers* (Matthew 5:9); and Paul said, *Indeed, true companion, I ask you also to help these women* (Philippians 4:3)—to come alongside them and help them just as a story from Luke tells of a big catch of fish and some from another boat who came alongside and helped them: *And they beckoned unto their partners, which were in the other ship, that they should come and help them. And they came, and filled both the ships* (Luke 5:7).

We often get our problems so tangled up and our pride so involved in the argument that things go so far we are not able to solve the problem ourselves. We need a peacemaker.

The questions we must ask ourselves are whether we are a troublemaker or a peacemaker, a source of confusion or a source of reconciliation, and the kind of individual others can turn to for help. It is not an easy job being a peacemaker. It can actually be a dangerous job because sometimes the fire will fall on the one trying to help others.

Help these women. We may wonder how the true companion went about this assignment. We could imagine that perhaps after the reading of the letter and things had settled a bit, the peacemaker said, "Euodia and Syntyche, I want both of you to come over to my house for supper Friday night."

One of them may have said, "Well, I don't know if I can be in the same room with her or not," while the other said, "After what she said to me, I don't know if I can be in the same room with her either." The true companion responded, "Come on—do it for Jesus and for Paul."

They gave in and went to the true companion's house. We can imagine the atmosphere when they both got there. The true companion said, "Euodia, I remember the Sunday you got saved; and Syntyche, I remember that you were at the altar with her and personally led her to faith in Jesus." Tears began to well up in Euodia's eyes.

"Ladies, I remember when you used to go visiting together and what a joy it was on Sunday mornings to see the two of you in the congregation with smiles on your faces. When the invitation was given, you walked down the aisle with someone you had led to Christ. Euodia and Syntyche, let's get down on our knees and thank the Lord for all of the good things He has done for us and for His goodness to us, for saving us, and for putting up with us and all of our faults and failures."

They got down on their knees; and when it was over, they embraced one another. The spiritual atmosphere was instantly changed.

We must ask ourselves if there is anyone in the church with whom we have a problem and then make an effort settle the matter. A question immediately arises: "But I don't know how they will respond." It does not matter how they respond. As poet Mary H. Waldrip said, "A little explained, a little endured, a little forgiven, the problem is cured."

AN ASK FOR AN ETERNAL PERSPECTIVE

Paul articulated one of the greatest statements of all time when he spoke of those *whose names are in the book of life* (Philippians

4:3). When people come to the decision to receive the Lord Jesus Christ as their Savior, their name is inscribed indubitably by the blood of Jesus in *the Lamb's book of life* (Revelation 21:27).

There is only one way to have our names written in the Lamb's book of life,

Remember back to the days of taking examinations. We would always want to know how we did—whether we passed or failed. Sometimes in college, the professor would post the grades on his office door, and we would go as soon as possible to see if our name was on the list of those who had passed.

The scope. As we think of the Lamb's book of life, we may wonder if our name is written there. Some of the most heart-wrenching words in the Bible are found in Revelation 20:15—*if anyone's name was not found written in the book of life, he was thrown into the lake of fire.* John, the Revelator, used the word *anyone.* There are no exceptions.

The salvation. There is only one way to have our names written in the Lamb's book of life, and that is by coming to Christ and being born again.

The sentence. Every person whose name is not written in the Lamb's book of life will be cast into the lake of fire. To be forever lost with Satan and his fallen angels and without the forgiveness of sin is beyond description.

If we are saved, we must shout and thank the Lord for His forgiveness and the promise of eternal life. We must pray and ask the Lord to use us to win the lost to make hell smaller and heaven larger. We need churches filled with the sweet aroma of salvation and saints who are committed to loving each other and this lost and dying world.

19

THE MENTAL MAKEOVER

We are going to have a checkup from the neck up and discover how to get our thinking and minds right. Many people need a spiritual formula to deal with depression, anger, resentment self-pity, worry, and fear.

The letter to the Philippians was written from Mamertine Prison, but it sounds as though Paul wrote it from a luxurious hotel. We almost expect him to say at the end, "I wish you were here."

There is more than one type of prison.

Paul's writing a letter from prison impacts us because there is more than one type of prison. Iron bars make a prison, but there are other things that make a prison also. There are those who live in a dungeon of despair and others behind walls of worry. Some are shackled with chains of poor health while others know the iron bars of disappointment, the chains of circumstances, and the fetters of fear. What Paul has to say is incredibly relevant even in our day.

Since Paul knows he cannot get out of prison, he decides that "If I'm here, I might as well remodel the place." He does so but on the inside, not the outside. *Not that I speak from want, for I have learned to be content in whatever circumstances I am* (Philippians 4:11).

There are five principles to the peace of God:

Rejoice in the Lord always; again I will say, rejoice! Let your gentle spirit be known to all men. The Lord is near. Be anxious for nothing, but in everything by prayer and supplication with thanksgiving let your requests be made known to God. And the peace of God, which surpasses all comprehension, will guard your hearts and your minds in Christ Jesus. Finally, brethren, whatever is true, whatever is honorable, whatever is right, whatever is pure, whatever is lovely, whatever is of good repute, if there is any excellence and if anything worthy of praise, dwell on these things. The things you have learned and received and heard and seen in me, practice these things, and the God of peace will be with you (Philippians 4:4-9).

REJOICE IN THE PRESENCE OF THE LORD

The first principle to peace is to learn to rejoice in the presence of the Lord: *Rejoice in the Lord always; again I will say, rejoice! Let your gentle spirit be known to all men. The Lord is near* (Philippians 4:4-5).

Paul was not in that prison by himself; the Lord was with him. Consequently, step one is to rejoice in the presence of the Lord. Paul expressed an incredible thought: *The Lord is near* (Philippians 4:5). Paul did not mean that the Second Coming of the Lord was near but that "the Lord is here; the Lord is at hand. I am in this prison; but I'm here with Jesus and I rejoice in the Lord." What an incredible thing for us to learn—that no matter where we are, how lonely the night, how dark the road, how dismal the prison, or how big the problem, Jesus Christ is always there.

The joy of the Lord is a thermostat, not a thermometer.

The only way we can understand this is when he says, *Rejoice in the Lord always* (Philippians 4:4). We do not rejoice in our circumstances or that we have been put in a prison with vermin, deprivation, suffering, and cold. Absolutely not! It is the fact that nothing *will be able to separate us from the love of God, which is in Christ Jesus our Lord* (Romans 8:39). This joy is to be continual, not a sometimes thing. *Rejoice in the Lord always* literally means to "rejoice all the time."

The joy of the Lord is a thermostat, not a thermometer. A thermometer registers conditions; a thermostat controls them. Happiness is related to the thermometer. If our hap is good, we are happy; if our hap is bad, we are unhappy. Our condition of happiness goes up and down with our circumstances, but joy remains constant because Jesus is constant. We must learn to practice the presence of God and understand that He is always there in whatever circumstance we find ourselves. Our desire should not be to become a thermometer but to set the thermostat. If we do not have joy, it is because Jesus is not real to us.

When Jesus was facing the cross, He spoke of His joy: *At that very time He rejoiced greatly in the Holy Spirit, and said, "I praise You, O Father, Lord of heaven and earth, that You have hidden these things from the wise and intelligent and have revealed them to infants. Yes, Father, for this way was well-pleasing in Your sight"* (Luke 10:21). Before He was crucified, He told His disciples, *These things I have spoken to you so that My joy may be in you, and that your joy may be made full* (John 15:11). *You will make known to me the path of life; In Your presence is fullness of joy; In Your right hand there are pleasures forever* (Psalm 16:11).

The Apostle Paul said, "They have locked me in, but they can't lock Jesus out"—*Rejoice in the Lord always . . . The Lord is near* (Philippians 4:4,5). If we want to have a good mental attitude, we will find joy in Jesus and not in circumstances because circumstances change but Jesus never changes. We can never be shut away from Him. *Rejoice in the Lord always* because He is always with us. He will never leave us nor forsake us (Hebrews 13:5). We must set the Lord before our face and consider Him, contemplate Him, praise Him, love Him, and enjoy Him. Do not rejoice in circumstances; rejoice in the Lord.

RELY ON THE POWER OF GOD

We need to rely on the power of the Lord for Paul said to *be anxious for nothing, but in everything by prayer and supplication with thanksgiving let your requests be made known to God* (Philippians 4:6). If we have a problem, we are to tell God about it: *in everything by prayer and supplication with thanksgiving*. We are not to worry about anything.

Worry is **worthless** as well as one of the most damaging emotions we face. Worry will do the same thing to us mentally that sand will do to machinery. There are few things that hurt our body more than worry. We should not look down on the one who overeats or smokes cigarettes or drinks alcohol or takes drugs if we are given over to worry. Worry is a form of dissipation and gives rise to the idea of being pulled apart. On one hand is hope, and on the other hand is fear, and we can be pulled between hope and fear.

Jesus emphatically warned us against worry: *Who of you by being worried can add a single hour to his life?* (Matthew 6:27). The very best thing we could say about worry is that it does no good. Four times in Matthew 6 Jesus says, *Do not be worried; why are you worried;* or *do not worry*. It is not foresight but foreboding when we worry about things that are in the future. It is like a rocking chair; it gives us something to do but gets us nowhere.

***Worry does not take the sorrow out of tomorrow;
it takes the joy out of today.***

Behavioral psychologists tell us that 40 percent of what we worry about never happens, 30 percent has already happened and worry cannot change it, 12 percent is needless worry about health issues; and 10 percent is miscellaneous matters that do not deserve worry. Approximately 8 percent of the things that remain can be counted worthy of worry, and those can be divided into two categories: Those we can do something about and those we can do nothing about. If we can do something about them, then we should and quit worrying. If we can do nothing about them, worry will make no difference.

Worry is **wasteful**. Jesus said, *Do not worry about tomorrow; for tomorrow will care for itself* (Matthew 6:34). Worry does not take the sorrow out of tomorrow; it takes the joy out of today. Worry pulls tomorrow's clouds over today's sunshine. Worry does not help us get ready for tomorrow because God does not give us strength for tomorrow. *According to your days, so will your leisurely walk be* (Deuteronomy 33:25).

When we bring tomorrow's troubles into today, we overload today. Worry is the interest we pay on borrowed trouble. When we get to tomorrow, we are less ready because we arrive out of breath because we are trying to use today's strength for tomorrow's troubles. Consequently, we are overloaded today and worn out before we get to tomorrow.

Worry is **wicked**. Jesus said this was the way of the Gentiles: *For the Gentiles eagerly seek all these things* (Matthew 6:32). It is pagan behavior.

Paul did not say, "Don't worry," in a cavalier way. He told us exactly what to do: *Be anxious for nothing, but in everything by prayer and supplication with thanksgiving let your requests be made known to God* (Philippians 4:6). Worry about nothing; pray about everything.

Biblical peace is not the subtraction of problems from life but the addition of power to meet them.

The cure for worry is prayer to the God who is with us. It is prayer that is a place of power, provision, and peace. Unlock the morning with prayer. Refuse to worry: *In everything by prayer and supplication*. If a problem is big enough to concern us, it is big enough to concern God. We must never get the idea that some things are too small to tell God about: *In everything by prayer and supplication*.

We often think we need God for the big things when, in reality, we need God for everything. *Be anxious for nothing, but in everything by prayer and supplication with thanksgiving let your requests be made known to God* (Philippians 4:6). We may think, "But I don't want to bother Him with the little stuff." There is nothing big to God. It is all little stuff to Him, and He is concerned.

REFLECT ON THE PROVISION OF THE LORD

Paul said that when we ask God to help us, to do it with thanksgiving. *Be anxious for nothing . . . with thanksgiving let your requests be made known to God* (Philippians 4:6). If we ask God for more and do not thank Him for what He has already done, it is unlikely that we will get our prayers answered as we would hope.

There is no higher expression of faith than thanksgiving, and worry is the highest expression of unbelief. We must refuse to worry and tell God about it instead. We must thank God for what He has done and for what He is going to do. Paul was encouraging a spirit of thanksgiving while he was in a slimy dungeon, and he did that because of the blessings he had. Sometimes we just need to get things in focus. We begin to feel sorry for ourselves and fail to understand the blessings of God.

We must not take things for granted but with gratitude. *Blessed be the Lord, who daily bears our burden, the God who is our salvation. Selah* (Psalm 68:19). *Selah* means, "think about that." *The LORD's lovingkindnesses indeed never cease, for His compassions never fail. They are new every morning; great is Your faithfulness* (Lamentations 3:22-23).

Thank Him. If we are in a dungeon, thank Him for our spiritual blessings and the simple blessings. Unthankful people are always unhappy people. Rather than being humbly grateful, some people are grumbly hateful and are filled with bitterness, fear, negativism, selfishness, and self-pity.

REST IN THE PEACE OF THE LORD

And the peace of God, which surpasses all comprehension, will guard your hearts and your minds in Christ Jesus (Philippians 4:7).

Because Paul was a very important prisoner, he most likely was surrounded by Roman guards day and night; however, he knew that he had the joy of the Lord to gladden him and the peace of God to guard him, not the peace of circumstances, for Christ was in the prison with him.

Biblical peace is not the subtraction of problems from life but the addition of power to meet them. We do not keep this peace;

this peace keeps us. It is a peace that passes our own understanding. We cannot get it from a bottle, a syringe, a psychiatrist, a psychologist, a well-meaning friend, or a book. Jesus said, *Peace I leave with you; My peace I give to you* (John 14:27). It is peace that the world cannot give and the world cannot take away. We can only find our peace in Christ. *The steadfast of mind you will keep in perfect peace, because he trusts in You* (Isaiah 26:3).

RENEW IN THE PURPOSE OF GOD

Paul wrote of God's purpose: *Finally, brethren, whatever is true, whatever is honorable, whatever is right, whatever is pure, whatever is lovely, whatever is of good repute, if there is any excellence and if anything worthy of praise, dwell on these things* (Philippians 4:8). We can choose our thoughts just like we can choose our friends.

We can choose our thoughts just like we can choose our friends.

We can be selective as to what gets into our mind. We can allow filth, debauchery, and negativism into our mind or we can say, "There's no room in my mind for such."

How are we going to think the right things or how are we not going to think the wrong things? Simply by thinking the right things. We are *fearfully and wonderfully made* (Psalm 139:14), but we cannot think two thoughts at the same time. Therefore, if we are thinking what we ought to be thinking, we will not be thinking what we ought not to be thinking. The cure for "stinking thinking" is to think on the right things.

There are six tests regarding whatever we admit into our mind.

The Reliance Test

The reliance test asks the questions, "Is it true? Can we bank on it? Can we rely on it?" It must be *whatever is true* (Philippians 4:8). Today's generation does not ask, "Is it true?" but "Does it work?" We must not let anything come into our thoughts and life and consciously dwell there nor absorb it into our heart and our philosophy if it is not based on biblical truth. We must not dwell on it or allow it to become a part of our thought patterns.

The Respect Test

The respect test asks the question, "Is it honorable?" *Whatever is honorable"* (Philippians 4:8). We must not let dishonorable things into our mind. There are things that are not worthy of our respect or worthy of our time. Some things are not bad because they are vile but because they are inane—silly and stupid.

The Rightness Test

The rightness test asks the question, "Is it right?" *Whatever is right* (Philippians 4:8)—whatever things are "straight" as opposed to "crooked." We are not to let any *crooked* thinking come into our mind; but unfortunately, many let things come in that are crooked. They do not necessarily lay down a measuring rod but just kind of go this way and that way a bit. Paul said there are certain things that should not get through the gate—things that are unreliable, disrespectful, or untrue.

The Reverence Test

The reverence test asks the question, "Could this be offered to God?" *Whatever is pure* (Philippians 4:8)—pure meaning "free of contamination."

When Paul said, *"Whatever is pure,"* he was asking if it was something we would not be ashamed to offer to the Lord whether it was a story, a movie, a friendship, or a relationship and say, "Lord, I offer it to you and worship you with it." Some would say we are not supposed to worship God with everything;

however, Paul said, *Whether, then, you eat or drink or whatever you do, do all to the glory of God* (1 Corinthians 10:31).

If there is anything we are doing that cannot pass the reverence test—any relationship, activity, meal, recreation, or business deal, then we should not let it into our mind.

The Relationship Test

The relationship test asks the question, "Does this thought move me toward love?" *Whatever is lovely* (Philippians 4:8). The word *lovely* does not mean "beautiful" but "to cause you to love" or "toward love." If something that comes into our mind that causes us to criticize unjustly or bring division, it is wrong although it does not mean that we must approve of what other people do.

The Refinement Test

The refinement test asks the question, "Are these things that we ought to allow at the gate of our mind?" *Whatever is of good repute* (Philippians 4:8) or things that are "high-toned" or "favorably known." No doubt every church has a few gossips. They use their ears as garbage cans and love to listen to ideas that are not commendable. They allow these things to track mud on the carpet of their mind rather than not allowing them to come in.

Paul wrapped it up by saying, *If there is any excellence and if anything worthy of praise, dwell on these things* (Philippians 4:8). We can absolutely take back conquered ground and say, "I'm only going to let these types of thoughts in my mind."

We do not have to think about anything we do not want to think about. However, everyone is thinking about something. We cannot control our thought life by keeping our mind in neutral. If we are not thinking something right, we are going to be thinking something wrong. If we are not thinking something good, we are going to be thinking something bad; and the way not to think bad thoughts is not by trying not to think bad thoughts. For example, try not to think of a submarine. We instantly picture one in our mind, and the only way not to think about a submarine is not by trying not to think about it but by thinking about something else. People who are trying not to think about a submarine are thinking about the submarine they are trying not to think about.

We can absolutely take back conquered ground.

We must learn to think God's thoughts after Him. Paul's standard in Philippians 4 was the grid through which everything must come before it finds lodging in our mind. *The things you have learned and received and heard and seen in me, practice these things, and the God of peace will be with you* (Philippians 4:9).

If we follow Paul's teaching regarding *true, honorable, right, pure, lovely,* and *good repute,* we will have the peace of God in our heart.

THE PROVISIONS OF THE CHRISTIAN LIFE (PHILIPPIANS 4:10-23)

20

THE COMMUNITY OF CONTENTMENT

Contentment is a great treasure. It softens our privations, sweetens our provisions, and makes a cottage as fair as a castle. Many people have a restlessness, an uneasiness, and a dissatisfaction in their life and are searching for contentment.

A Quaker once wanted to teach a lesson to his neighbors and announced that he was going to give one of his lots of land to the most contented person in the village. One day a man came and knocked on his door to collect the lot. The Quaker said to him, "Art thee a contented person?" The man said, "I am" to which the Quaker responded, "If thou art content, then why dost thee want my lot?"

Unfortunately, many people are not content but are filled with complaints and always striving for more. They complain if the children are noisy rather than being grateful that they are healthy and happy. They lament their jobs when many people are too ill to work. They are discontent because they do not have a "fine" car or their house is not located in the best neighborhood in town. At the same time, there are many people in the world who have never owned a car much less a house.

The Apostle Paul found the secret of contentment:

> *But I rejoiced in the Lord greatly, that now at last you have revived your concern for me; indeed, you were concerned before, but you lacked opportunity. Not that I speak from want, for I have learned to be content in whatever circumstances I am. I know how to get along with humble means, and I also know how to live in prosperity; in any and every circumstance I have learned the secret of being filled and going hungry, both of having abundance and suffering need. I can do all things through Him who strengthens me* (Philippians 4:10-13).

Paul said *I know* and *I have learned* (Philippians 4:12)—he came to *know* by experience. The word "learn" is one Paul took right out of the mystery religions of his day. It was a word that meant "to be initiated" because in those days people would be initiated into the mystery religions. They were told that as members, they would possess insight and secret information into deep, divine truths and would be able to "know" those truths. Paul borrows that word when he says, "I have been initiated and am a member of the community of the contented."

There are qualifications to enter a level of life of the community of the contented that most never discover.

WE SHOULD REJOICE IN OUR PROVISIONS.

The first secret we learn from the words of the Apostle Paul is that if we want to be in the secret society of the contented, we must learn to rejoice in our substance—in what we have. *But I rejoiced in the Lord greatly* (Philippians 4:10). God met Paul's needs in a special way. In fact, the whole background of the Book of Philippians is based on the fact that the believers in Philippi had been sending special gifts to Paul and were sharing in his ministry through the gifts they sent. However, it may have been about 10 years since they had sent Paul a gift. It was not that they did not love him or care for him or were not concerned about him but that they *lacked opportunity* (Philippians 4:10). They now had revived their concern, their interest, and their fellowship in the gospel with Paul just like beautiful flowers blossoming again in the springtime.

Many people are not content but are filled with complaints and always striving for more.

God knows our needs and is able to meet those needs. *I know how to get along with humble means, and I also know how to live in prosperity* (Philippians 4:12). He knew what it was like to have little as well as what it was like to have more than sufficient. Regardless of his circumstances, Paul was a man who had needs just like everyone does.

We sometimes idealize people in the Bible and forget they were real-life human beings. Paul snored and sneezed and scratched just like people do today. He had to have food and clothing just as we do; and Paul realized that God knew his needs because Jesus said, *Your heavenly Father knows that you need all these things* (Matthew 6:32).

God sometimes meets our needs in unusual ways. He did it for Elijah when Elijah hid in the Kerith Ravine and *the ravens brought him bread and meat in the morning and bread and meat in the evening, and he drank from the brook* (1 Kings 17:6). God could have met Paul's needs directly out of heaven, but He used the faithfulness and the generosity of the Philippian believers. Paul said, *You have revived your concern for me* (Philippians 4:10). When God gives us an opportunity to be a blessing in the lives of others, He wants us to take advantage of that opportunity. *So then, while we have opportunity, let us do good to all people, and especially to those who are of the household of the faith* (Galatians 6:10).

Thank God for whatever He has provided, praise Him for it, and serve Him in the midst of it.

When it comes to contentment, Paul was basically saying, "I have learned to rejoice in whatever God provides in my life." We should also rejoice in our provisions whether they be a little or a lot. How much does it take for us to be satisfied? How many gadgets do we need? What kind of car do we have to have in order to be happy? What size house do we have to own in order to be satisfied? If we want to learn the steps into the community of the contented, we need to learn to thank God for whatever He has provided, praise Him for it, and serve Him in the midst of it.

Shortly before Mother Theresa's death at age 87, she said, "You will never know that Jesus is all you need until all you have is Jesus." When she passed away, all she owned was a bucket and two saris. She came to learn that Jesus was all she needed in this life. Jesus gives more than satisfaction; He also gives contentment.

WE SHOULD REST IN OUR POSSESSIONS.

We need to rest in whatever condition we are in or rest in our situation. Paul was a man who was contented in his situation. There was not a sense of frenzy or unease in his life for he wrote, *I have learned to be content in whatever circumstances I am* (Philippians 4:11).

What does it mean to be content?

THE COMMUNITY OF CONTENTMENT

Self-Satisfaction

Some think that to be content means we are totally satisfied and have no ambition whatsoever. However, the Bible teaches there is a place for sanctified ambition—a place for a desire to be everything that we can possibly be.

None of us should be content to be mediocre Christians when we could be on fire and shake the world for Jesus Christ.

It is unthinkable for someone to be content making C's in school when they can make A's. It is unthinkable for someone to be content being an office clerk in a business when they could be the president of the business. It is unthinkable for someone to be content being third string when they could be All American. None of us should be content to be mediocre Christians when we could be on fire and shake the world for Jesus Christ.

Self-Sufficiency

We should have a sanctified discontent in our life. Paul was not talking about self-sufficiency when he said, *I have learned to be content in whatever circumstances I am.*

Some people believe they can handle everything themselves. This is often reflected when motivation speakers say we have all we need within us to be successful and all we need to do is put our mind and our skills to work to become self-sufficient. However, every person alive is just one heartbeat away from eternity. We are not in control. We are not self-sufficient.

Paul carefully chose a word found in the world in which he lived—a word taken from stoic philosophers that meant self-sufficiency. The stoic philosophers took this particular Greek word and used it to describe getting to the state of mind where a person was totally unmoved by outward circumstances, kept everything on the inside, and did not need anything or anyone. They were totally oblivious to any needs outside their own life or anyone who could do something for them. They were totally self-sufficient in their own strength.

The stoic's mindset was they were not moved by anything. They stressed that a person had to get to the point where they had no emotions whatsoever and be totally unmoved by anything. In other words, if they broke a plate, they said, "I don't care." If they lost a pet, they said, "I don't care." If they lost a loved one, they said, "I don't care." There is only one problem with that philosophy. We do care! This was not what Paul was talking about. He was not talking about self-satisfaction or self-sufficiency.

Savior-Sufficiency

Paul had a habit of taking words from the secular world in which he lived and baptizing them into the Christian faith. He does that very thing to this Greek term. He said, *I have learned to be content in whatever circumstances I am.* The word literally means to be self-contained. In other words, we are not dependent on outward circumstances because we are drawing on inward strengths and realities. For instance, it was used to describe a land or country that was self-contained and did not have any imports to meet the needs of its citizens.

Paul was saying, "I have found a secret. The secret of contentment is not something you get from the outside. It is not the circumstances and situations of life; rather, it is a sufficiency that comes from within." He was talking about a Savior sufficiency—the presence of Jesus Christ in our heart and life.

When we have Jesus and understand that in Christ is everything we need to meet every situation in life, then we are on our way to contentment. If we learn that secret and learn to rest in our situation because of inner resources by the presence of God in our life, then we can accept our circumstances.

Accept Our Situation

Paul was in jail yet he accepted this circumstance. Many people go through life and are constantly whining about their circumstances. Nothing is ever quite right. They are like wounded animals that are constantly gnawing and pawing at the trap of circumstances in their life. However, they can come to the point where they accept those circumstances.

It is more difficult for people to adjust to plenty than to little.

A man went through a garden one day and saw the oak tree and the pine tree both moping and groaning. He said to the oak tree, "What's wrong with you?" The oak tree said, "I'm so dissatisfied. I'm not tall and stately like the pine." He went over to the pine tree and it was moping also. He said, "What's wrong with you?" The pine tree said, "I'm not wide and fragrant like the peach tree." The man went to the little violet that was just sitting there shining and smiling. The man said to the little violet, "Why are you so happy and so contented to be a violet?" The violet said, "If God had wanted me to be an oak tree, He would have made me one. If God had wanted me to be a pine tree, He would have made me one. Evidently, God wanted me to be a violet; and I've decided that I'm going to be the very best violet I can be."

Adapt to Our Surroundings

We must also adapt to our surroundings. Paul said, *I know how to get along with humble means, and I also know how to live in prosperity; in any and every circumstance I have learned the secret of being filled and going hungry, both of having abundance and suffering need* (Philippians 4:12). Paul was saying that when he did not have much, he learned to adapt to that; and when he had a lot, he learned how to adapt to that as well.

It seems, however, that it is more difficult for people to adjust to plenty than to little. One of the most dangerous things that can happen is to become prosperous because if we do not understand that our circumstances are opportunities to praise the Lord and live for the Lord whatever that may be, then we are in trouble.

There is victory over every temptation, grace for every trouble, and power and strength for every need.

If we are in lowly circumstances, then we must keep in mind that the true riches are in Jesus. If we are in prosperous circumstances, we must keep in mind that none of those things can bring the real joy that Jesus can bring into our life.

Appropriate Our Success

By appropriating our success, we are to use whatever situation we are in as an opportunity to tell someone about Jesus.

Paul appropriated his jail situation as an opportunity to tell people about Christ. *Now I want you to know, brethren, that my circumstances have turned out for the greater progress of the gospel so that my imprisonment in the cause of Christ has become well known throughout the whole praetorian guard and to everyone else* (Philippians 1:12-13). *All the saints greet you, especially those of Caesar's household* (Philippians 4:22).

Paul said that the very fact that he was in jail gave him an opportunity to further the gospel of Jesus Christ and to get the message of Jesus to places he never could have taken it had those circumstances not come to pass.

If we will determine with the help of God to take whatever our circumstances are and use them as opportunities to tell others about Jesus, we will be on our way to becoming a member of the community of contentment.

WE SHOULD REALIZE OUR POWER.

The crescendo is when Paul gave us one of the greatest promises in the Bible: *I can do all things through Him who strengthens me* (Philippians 4:13). Had Paul said "I can't," it would have been the language of pessimism because the pessimist says, "I don't think it can be done," while the optimist says, "I think it can be done."

We Move From Pessimism

We have a lot of language of pessimism. Churches get into the language of pessimism saying, "We just can't do it. We can't grow. We can't reach people for the Lord. We just can't be the kind of church we ought to be." Christians get into the language of pessimism as well when they say, "I just can't grow in the Lord. I can't be a witness for the Lord. I can't understand the Bible. I can't pray."

We Move From Presumption

Paul did not say, "I can't," nor did he say, "I can." That would have been the language of presumption.

A new Christian was reading the New Testament through and got to Philippians 4:13. In his Bible, the verse was located on the bottom on the right side of the right page. He read the words, *I can do all things*, and immediately thought, "Oh, Paul, you've gone too far now." However, when he turned the page, he read the rest of it: *through Him who strengthens me.*

We Move to Power

I can do all things through Him who strengthens me is the language of the power of the indwelling Christ in our life, and we can claim the promise. There is victory over every temptation, grace for every trouble, and power and strength for every need.

I can do all things through Him who strengthens me literally means "through the One who is constantly infusing His power in me." As a child of God, the living Lord Jesus dwells in our heart and life; and there is available power to be everything God wants us to be and do whatever God wants us to do no matter the circumstances, the adversities, the problems, or the needs. Whatever we are facing, we can do all those things through Jesus Christ who strengthens us.

Rejoice in your provisions, rest in your possessions, and realize your power in Christ.

Many people do not know how to cope so they succumb to life's pressures, difficulties, and reversals because they never developed coping skills. However, in Christ, there is power to cope and meet the problems of life head-on.

A man lived his entire life on a meager little farm, barely eking out a living from the soil. Shortly after he died, oil was discovered on his property. The man was living on top of a fortune and never even knew it was there.

We should not be satisfied to go through life whining, complaining, moaning, and groaning when God has given us a fortune in the presence and power of the Lord Jesus Christ. We can be content because we can realize the strength God has provided for us.

My late father was a member of the community of contentment. He knew what it was to live in poverty and in prosperity. He knew what it was to build a successful business, to see Hurricane Frederic wipe it out in 1979, and then to rebuild it again. He knew what it was to love his wife and lead her into her eternal rest with Christ. However, I never remember hearing him complain and gripe about life and its challenges. I only remember one time that he even raised his voice. My brother and I were arguing; and he came into the family room where we were and said, "Sit down. If you boys could ever learn to work together, you could help change the world." I never forgot it.

Become a member of the community of contentment and rejoice in your provisions, rest in your possessions, and realize your power in Christ.

21

ACCORDING TO GOD'S RICHES IN GLORY

The final words of Paul to his beloved Philippian church form a thank you for the gift they sent to him. A case could possibly be built that the church at Philippi was the favorite of all the churches he established.

I thank my God in all my remembrance of you (Philippians 1:3). They were a source of constant gratitude and thanksgiving. Paul later wrote, *My beloved brethren whom I long to see, my joy and crown* (Philippians 4:1). He was writing to these greatly loved people of God whom he had been able to establish in Christ and thanking them for the gracious gift which they had sent to him.

It is important that we learn the grace of gratitude—to say thank you, particularly when someone does something for us. It is always good to drop a note in the mail expressing our thanks. Paul's final words are a "thank you" for the gift that the believers of Philippi had sent to him but also rather like a "receipt."

I have received everything in full and have an abundance; I am amply supplied (Philippians 4:18). The phrases used were ones often expressed in business transactions. He would probably never be in Philippi again so he was businesslike in his dealings in noting that "You have given to my future ministry, and I am sending you this receipt." They were in the business of spreading the gospel together, and Paul remarked to them that *no church shared with me in the matter of giving and receiving but you alone* (Philippians 4:15).

It is important that we learn the grace of gratitude.

Another amazing truth noted in the Book of Philippians is how God meets the needs of our life. Jesus said that *your heavenly Father knows that you need all these things* (Matthew 6:32), and God is the great provider of those needs.

WE NEED TO INVEST IN THE BEAUTY OF GIVING.

Speaking of the gift from the church at Philippi, Paul said they had done well. The Bible teaches the beauty of giving. Jesus said, *Freely you received, freely give* (Matthew 10:8). Paul also quoted the words of Jesus: *It is more blessed to give than to receive* (Acts 20:35).

The Apostle Paul had ministered in Philippi, had won people to faith in the Lord Jesus Christ, and had now gone forward in his journey. From time to time, the Philippians sent gifts to Paul. A beautiful thing—the beauty of giving. Paul told us why it is such a beautiful thing to be a giver.

Blesses Others

The first benefit of being a giver is that it blesses others. Because of their faithfulness in giving, Paul's needs were supplied which made it possible for him to preach the gospel and tell others about the Lord Jesus Christ.

God's way of meeting needs and encouraging others is by using people. The gift from the church at Philippi was such a blessing to Paul that he said, *At the first preaching of the gospel, after I left Macedonia* [where Philippi was located], *no church shared with me in the matter of giving and receiving but you alone* (Philippians 4:15). Paul had established a number of churches, but no other churches supported his ministry. Paul's words indicated a note of **sadness** but also a note of **gladness**. When he said *but you alone*, he was very grateful for their generosity in giving.

There are two kinds of churches and two kinds of Christians. They are either like a cistern or a spring. A cistern takes water in and holds it—it has no outlet—while a spring gives out water.

Some churches are merely cisterns. All that interests them is doing what they want to do locally. The same thing is true about Christians. Some Christians are only interested in receiving—what they can get out if it and how it will help or benefit them. On the other hand, other churches and Christians are like a spring—constantly giving and sharing with others.

The first beauty of giving is that it blesses others.

Enriches Us

Giving also enriches us. *Not that I seek the gift itself* (Philippians 4:17). The point is not that we get something *but that I seek for the profit which increases to your account* (Philippians 4:17). Paul was interested in the welfare and spiritual growth of the people at the church in Philippi and knew they would be blessed and enriched because of their giving. When we learn to be a giver, we become a blessing as well as receive a blessing.

Not only does giving enrich us on earth but also in heaven. Jesus said, *Do not store up for yourselves treasures on earth . . . But store up for yourselves treasures in heaven* (Matthew 6:19-20). When people on earth die, what do they leave behind? Everything. It is impossible to translate material things on earth into the coinage of heaven, but we can be rich in heaven through our giving on earth.

It is impossible to translate material things on earth into the coinage of heaven.

George W. Truett was pastor of First Baptist Church, Dallas, Texas, from 1897-1944 and the president of the Southern Baptist Convention from 1927-1929. He was one of the most famous Southern Baptist preachers and writers of his era. A very wealthy rancher once took him out to see his land. "Preacher, I own everything as far as you can see—everything in front of you, behind you, and all around you. I own it." The preacher said, "That's wonderful, my friend, but how much do you own in heaven?"

Pleases God

The beauty of giving is that it blesses others, enriches us, and pleases God. *I am amply supplied, having received from Epaphroditus what you have sent, a fragrant aroma, an acceptable sacrifice, well-pleasing to God* (Philippians 4:18).

One of the ways to really understand the message of the Bible is to see the beautiful pictures it paints, and Paul does this by taking us back to Old Testament terminology. In those days, there would be a priest who would take a sacrifice, put it on the altar, and put fragrance on the sacrifice. Some of the offerings required frankincense and some required oil. The sweet fragrance that God smelled from the smoke of the offerings did not come from the burning flesh of the animals but from the spices and seasonings that were added into the sacrifices.

Some of the sacrifices pictured the sin offering that Jesus would offer on the cross of Calvary. As the sweet fragrance would go up, the picture was that God would smell the fragrance and it would be pleasing and acceptable to Him.

Paul raised the whole matter of giving to another level. He said that when we make our offerings, we become like a priest putting a sacrifice on the altar and that gift goes up like a sweet fragrance that is pleasing to the Lord.

Every born-again child of God is a priest.

Every born-again child of God is a priest: *You also, as living stones, are being built up as a spiritual house for a holy priesthood* (1 Peter 2:5), and *You are a . . . royal* PRIESTHOOD (1 Peter 2:9). *To offer up spiritual sacrifices acceptable to God through Jesus Christ* (1 Peter 2:5). When we offer these sacrifices, God is pleased.

1. **Our Walk in Life**
   To offer up our very life as a sacrifice is total commitment to the Lord. *Therefore I urge you, brethren, by the mercies of God, to present your bodies a living and holy sacrifice, acceptable to God, which is your spiritual service of worship* (Romans 12:1).

2. **Our Worship to the Lord**
   When we praise the Lord, we are offering a sacrifice unto Him. When we sing hymns of praise, we are offering the fruit of our lips as a sacrifice. *Through Him then, let us continually offer up a sacrifice of praise to God, that is, the fruit of lips that give thanks to His name* (Hebrews 13:15).

3. **Our Winning of the Lost**
   When we win a soul to Christ, it is like an offering to the Lord and pleases Him. *To be a minister of Christ Jesus to the Gentiles, ministering as a priest the gospel of God, so that my offering of the Gentiles may become acceptable, sanctified by the Holy Spirit* (Romans 15:16).

WE NEED TO BE INSPIRED BY THE BOUNTY OF GOD.

And my God will supply all your needs according to His riches in glory in Christ Jesus (Philippians 4:19). This is one of the most wonderful promises in the Bible, but it must be kept in context. The previous verses talked about our giving to meet the needs of other people. In essence, Paul was saying, "Since you are being used of God to meet the needs of others, God will meet your needs." We cannot claim the promise of Philippians 4:19 until we have lived the beauty of giving.

The elements of that promise are:

The Source of Our Supply

And my God will supply all your needs. The eternal, immortal, awesome, wonderful, majestic God is the one who will supply our needs. He a fountain that continually flows, an ocean that will never run dry, and a warehouse that will always be full. There is a royal bank in heaven with eternal deposits and unlimited funds; and it has never experienced a depression or a recession. "My Father is rich in houses and lands, He holdeth the wealth of the world in His hands! Of rubies and diamonds, of silver and gold, His coffers are full, He has riches untold . . . But I've been adopted, my name's written down, an heir to a mansion, a robe and a crown" ("A Child of the King," Harriet Buell, 1877).

1. **Rich in Goodness**

    God's bank of heaven is rich in goodness. *Or do you think lightly of the riches of His kindness and tolerance and patience, not knowing that the kindness* [goodness KJV] *of God leads you to repentance?* (Romans 2:4).

2. **Rich in Grace**

    God is rich in grace, and we can never drain it dry. *In Him we have redemption through His blood, the forgiveness of our trespasses, according to the riches of His grace* (Ephesians 1:7).

3. Rich in Glory

God has a full supply of the riches of His glory. *I pray that the eyes of your heart may be enlightened, so that you will know what is the hope of His calling, what are the riches of the glory of His inheritance in the saints* (Ephesians 1:18).

One time a little girl misquoted the first verse of Psalm 23. Instead of saying, *The Lord is my shepherd, I shall not want*, she said "The Lord is my shepherd; that's all I want." She actually did not misquote it because if we have the Lord and if He is our shepherd and our God, then that is all we need. *My God shall supply all your need* (Philippians 4:19). He is the source of our supply.

The Scope of Our Supply

God's scope of our supply is rich. *My God shall supply all your need*—not just a few of our needs or a part of our needs or most of our needs but ALL of our needs. However, we sometimes get the idea that God is a cosmic bellboy; and all we have to do is just ring, and He will come running to do our bidding. *My God shall supply all your need*—not all our greed.

When I was a boy, Sears Roebuck and JCPenney's had large catalogs. Next to the Bible, those catalogs were the biggest books in our house. We would spend hours looking at the "wish" books. Many people think the Bible is just like those catalogs; however, God is not going to supply all our greed, but He will *supply all your need*.

1. Our Material Needs

God promised to supply our material needs because *your heavenly Father knows that you need all these things* (Matthew 6:32). God took care of the children of Israel for 40 years in the wilderness—an estimated 2.5 million of them. *Your clothes have not worn out on you, and your sandal has not worn out on your foot* (Deuteronomy 29:5).

2. **Our Emotional Needs**

   God promised to supply our emotional needs. Perhaps our heart is troubled, and we need peace. Jesus said, *Peace I leave with you; My peace I give to you; not as the world gives do I give to you. Do not let your heart be troubled, nor let it be fearful* (John 14:27). Perhaps our heart is broken. *He heals the brokenhearted and binds up their wounds* (Psalm 147:3).

3. **Our Spiritual Needs**

   God promised to supply our spiritual needs. Perhaps we need forgiveness of sin. *In Him we have redemption through His blood, the forgiveness of our trespasses* (Ephesians 1:7). Perhaps we need rest in our soul. Jesus said, *Come to Me, all who are weary and heavy-laden, and I will give you rest* (Matthew 11:28).

4. **Our Physical Needs**

   God promised to supply our physical needs. While Jesus was on the earth, He healed all sicknesses and diseases. There is no record that He healed only some of them; He healed all of them. There are mysteries in the miracles; however, we do know that *by His wounds you were healed* (1 Peter 2:24).

Therefore, since we have a great high priest who has passed through the heavens, Jesus the Son of God, let us hold fast our confession. For we do not have a high priest who cannot sympathize with our weaknesses, but One who has been tempted in all things as we are, yet without sin. Therefore let us draw near with confidence to the throne of grace, so that we may receive mercy and find grace to help in time of need (Hebrews 4:14-16).

We can walk boldly into the Holy of Holies and bring our needs to the Lord.

ACCORDING TO GOD'S RICHES IN GLORY

The Standard of Our Supply

The standard by which God meets our needs is *according to His riches in glory in Christ Jesus* (Philippians 4:19). The Bible is very careful about the prepositions it uses. It does not say, "My God shall supply all your need **out of** His riches in glory" but *according to His riches in glory*. What is the difference between out of and according to?

What we have to do with a check that meets our needs is cash it.

Suppose a man was to visit with Elon Musk, the founder of Tesla, and now the richest man in the world. Suppose this man goes to Mr. Musk and says, "Mr. Musk, I have a need, and I wonder if you would be willing to write me a check." Mr. Musk says, "Sure, I'll be happy to write you a check. I've got unlimited money. Here's a check for $5." What has Mr. Musk done? Written a check out of his riches, $5 worth out of his riches. However, suppose the man went to Elon Musk and told him his need; and Mr. Musk said, "Here's a blank check. Fill in whatever you need." That would not be out of his riches but according to his riches.

That is what Paul says concerning God in Philippians 4:19: *And my God will supply all your needs according to His riches in glory in Christ Jesus*. What should our response be? To claim it.

A man and his wife were in desperate circumstances and had no idea how they were going to make it when one day a check mysteriously appeared that would cover all of their needs. The man said to his wife, "Look at this check! It will take care of all of our needs. Let's put it in a frame and put it up on the wall. Let's write songs about it and sing about this wonderful check. Let's preach sermons about it and tell stories about it."

We would say, "That would be foolish." Exactly. What we have to do with a check that meets our needs is cash it. God is saying, "Cash this promise. Claim this promise." If we are faithful in our giving, we can ask God to supply all our needs according to His riches in glory!

WE NEED INTEREST IN THE BENEDICTION OF GRACE.

Paul closed the book of Philippians like he began it—with grace. *The grace of the Lord Jesus Christ be with your spirit* (Philippians 4:23).

Emancipating Grace

Paul wrote about grace and how it enabled and emancipated those in the church in Philippi. Many were slaves who worked in the palaces of the Caesars. Many of them were chained and shackled by sin. However, the message of grace came into their lives; and their shackles were broken and they were set free. "Every saint has a past, and every sinner has a future" (Oscar Wilde 1893).

Ennobling Grace

Paul also wrote about ennobling grace. *All the saints greet you, especially those of Caesar's household* (Philippians 4:22). They were slaves; yet through the grace of God, they were elevated to saints. God's grace elevates. A bumper sticker that was popular years ago read, "I must be somebody because God don't make no junk." We are somebody!

Enabling Grace

God's grace that saves us will also be God's grace that enables us. *The grace of the Lord Jesus Christ be with your spirit* (Philippians 4:23).

> *"Every saint has a past, and every sinner has a future."*

Anyone who would like to "get in on all of this" must start where the book starts. *Paul and Timothy, bond-servants of Christ Jesus, To all the saints in Christ Jesus* (Philippians 1:1). First, you must come to Christ. You must get "in" Christ Jesus. Then when you are "in" Christ Jesus, you have access to all of the wonderful truths God has made available for you. If you do not know Christ, then make Him Lord of your life today. If you do know Him, then recognize that you are "in" Christ and begin believing and living in His promises.

CONCLUSION

THE SAD CASE OF THE STOLEN SONG

There is a joy and peace that passes all understanding; but in order to walk in this joy and peace, we must embrace Christ daily and live in the power of the Holy Spirit.

God had given a land, a law, and a Lord to His ancient people Israel. They defiled the land, defied the law, and denied the Lord. As a result, the Babylonians came and carried them away to a strange land—a land of captivity. These people who were meant to sing lost their song.

> *By the rivers of Babylon, there we sat down and wept, when we remembered Zion. Upon the willows in the midst of it we hung our harps. For there our captors demanded of us songs, and our tormentors mirth, saying, "Sing us one of the songs of Zion." How can we sing the Lord's song in a foreign land?* (Psalm 137:1-4).

There was parakeet named Chippy. The young parakeet never saw it coming. One second, he was peacefully perched in his cage; and the next he was sucked in, washed up, and, blown over. The problems began when Chippy's owner decided to clean his cage with a vacuum cleaner. She removed the attachment from the end of the hose and stuck it in the cage. The phone rang, and she turned to pick it up.

They defiled the land, defied the law, and denied the Lord.

She had barely said hello when Chippy got sucked in. The bird's owner gasped, put down the phone, turned off the vacuum, and opened the bag. There was Chippy—alive but stunned. Since the bird was covered with dust and soot, she grabbed him up and raced to the bathroom, turned on the faucet, and held Chippy under the running water.

Then realizing that Chippy was soaked and shivering, she did what any compassionate bird owner would do—she reached for the hair dryer and blasted the parakeet with hot air. Poor Chippy never knew what hit him.

A few days after the trauma, the reporter who had initially written the story contacted Chippy's owner to see how the bird was recovering. "Well," she replied, "Chippy doesn't sing much anymore. He just sits and stares."

Millions of Christians have lost their song. Like Israel so long ago, they have been taken captive—not by the Babylonians but by the world, the flesh, and the devil. Babylon represents the world with its vanity, vexation, and vileness. Jerusalem represents salvation, the saints, and the songs. However, God's people had been taken captive; and as a result, they lost their song.

WE NEED TO REFRAIN FROM THE SAD MISERY OF A CAPTURED CHRISTIAN.

By the rivers of Babylon, there we sat down and wept, when we remembered Zion (Psalm 137:1). Misery. One of the ways we can tell that we truly know the Lord and have been saved and redeemed is if there is sadness and heartache when we are not in fellowship with God.

There are a lot of Christians who have been taken captive. God loves us too much to let us have joy and worldliness at the same time. We cannot have sin and joy in our heart at the same time. We often think the most miserable person in the world is an unsaved person when in reality the most miserable person in the world is a saved person who is out of fellowship with God.

Failure is often success at the wrong thing.

What is true joy? Not laughter. People can laugh and often do so to cover up the fact that they have no joy. They are laughing themselves into hell but will be unable to laugh their way out. Laughter is not joy nor is giddiness or happiness. In fact, happiness is like the surface of the sea. It depends upon which way the wind is blowing as to what the conditions will be for the sailors. However, the joy of the Lord is many fathoms deep where the winds never reach. It is a wonderful thing when joy and happiness merge; but when there is no happiness, we must thank God for the joy He gives to help us bear the pain.

Success does not bring joy, and failure is often success at the wrong thing. Success has a measure of diminishing returns. So-called successful people may "have it all" and yet still have no joy. Joy is that ecstasy of the soul that is at peace with God. It has been said that "joy is the flag that is flown from the castle of the heart when the king is in residence there." Joy is unspeakable and full of glory.

God loves us too much to let us live taken captive by the world, the flesh, and the devil and still have joy. God is the one who sometimes engineers sorrow.

Therefore thus says the LORD of hosts, "Because you have not obeyed My words, behold, I will send and take all the families of the north," declares the LORD, "and I will send to Nebuchadnezzar king of Babylon, My servant, and will bring them against this land and against its inhabitants and against all these nations round about; and I will utterly destroy them and make them a horror and a hissing, and an everlasting desolation. Moreover, I will take from them the voice of joy and the voice of gladness, the voice of the bridegroom and the voice of the bride, the sound of the millstones and the light of the lamp. This whole land will be a desolation and a horror, and these nations will serve the king of Babylon seventy years" (Jeremiah 25: 8-11).

God told them, "You would not hear my prophets so I am going to raise up this vile, wicked, and strong king; and he is going to carry you away into captivity. You will have no mirth, no joy, and no songs." God did this because He loved them—not because He did not love them.

Nebuchadnezzar was God's rattlesnake to bring the children of Israel to their senses. God had given them a land, a law, and a Lord...and had sent the prophets; however, they defiled the land, defied the law, and denied the Lord...and they wept.

WE NEED TO REFLECT ON THE STINGING MEMORY OF A CAPTURED CHRISTIAN.

By the rivers of Babylon, there we sat down and wept, when we remembered Zion (Psalm 137:1). They remembered Zion—the holy land, Jerusalem, the holy temple, the place of fellowship with God, the place of cleansing from sin; but now all they had was a stinging memory.

Are we out of fellowship with God yet still remember when we were in fellowship with Him—when God was so real; when worship was a thrill; when Jesus Christ was sweet and precious; and we could sing it, say it, and mean it?

If we do not love the Lord as much as we used to and do not walk in fellowship and know the sweet joy, glory, and presence of Jesus Christ in our heart, then we have been taken captive and our misery and our memory are inextricably interwoven.

WE NEED TO REMEMBER THE SARCASTIC MOCKERY OF A CAPTURED CHRISTIAN.

Upon the willows in the midst of it we hung our harps. For there our captors demanded of us songs, and our tormentors mirth, saying, "Sing us one of the songs of Zion" (Psalm 137:2-3). With great sarcasm, their captors commanded the captives to sing.

The world that hates Christians rejoices when they fall or stumble.

The devil delights to see a child of God fail or a scandal in the church or a child of God who lowers the banner and no longer has the cross before them and the world behind them.

The world hates us because we love the Lord Jesus Christ. Jesus said, *If you were of the world, the world would love its own; but because you are not of the world, but I chose you out of the world, because of this the world hates you* (John 15:19).

The world that hates Christians rejoices when they fall or stumble. *Sing us one of the songs of Zion*, they say.

We can sing to Babylon but never for Babylon. We have no right to sing the songs of Zion for this world that wants to blur the difference between the church and the world. They love to sing the songs of Zion in the bars. Every so often they will strike up the song, "Amazing Grace." At Christmastime, they will sing "Away in a Manager" while one week later they will be singing

"Auld Lang Syne" in a drunken brawl. *Sing us the songs of Zion* the people of Babylon said. They wanted Christians to become a mockery to the cause of the Lord and Savior Jesus Christ. God forbid that any of us should ever bring such blasphemy to Christ.

WE NEED TO REFUSE THE SILENCED MELODY OF A CAPTURED CHRISTIAN.

How can we sing the Lord's song in a foreign land? (Psalm 137:4). It is the Lord's song, a song of deliverance; and if it is a song of deliverance, how can we sing it when we have been taken captive? *You are my hiding place; You preserve me from trouble; You surround me with songs of deliverance* (Psalm 32:7).

The first recorded public song in the Bible was the song of deliverance when the children of Israel came out of Egypt, headed toward Canaan, crossed the Red Sea, and were set free from bondage. They sang the song of Moses and the Lamb—a song of deliverance: six hundred thousand male voices singing with the women singing the refrain. If we have been delivered, we cannot help but sing.

> *He brought me up out of the pit of destruction, out of the miry clay, and He set my feet upon a rock making my footsteps firm. He put a new song in my mouth, a song of praise to our God; many will see and fear and will trust in the Lord* (Psalm 40:2-3).

When God brings us up out of the pit, He puts our feet on the Rock; and we cannot help but sing. If we have been redeemed and delivered, there will be a song in our heart—the song of the soul set free.

What steals our song? Sorrow cannot. Jesus was facing dark Gethsemane and bloody Calvary; but before He and His disciples left the Upper Room after observing Passover, they sang *a*

CONCLUSION

hymn, [and] went out to the Mount of Olives (Matthew 26:30). Jesus sang in the midst of His sorrow.

Paul and Silas had their backs lacerated and were in stocks and bonds in the filth of the prison in Philippi (a former city in present-day Greece); *but about midnight Paul and Silas were praying and singing hymns of praise to God, and the prisoners were listening to them* (Acts 16:25).

We are not called to isolate ourselves from the world, but we can insulate ourselves in it!

We may experience dark nights or possibly an incurable disease. We may have wayward children or are between jobs and it looks bleak because now we are now past the age where people might be looking for someone with our skills. However, these things cannot steal our song because our joy does not depend upon what happens. We rejoice in the Lord!

As we come to the close of *The Joy Book: The Christian's Abundant Joy in the Darkest Days*, I would like to encourage all who have read this book to keep your joy by staying close to the Lord Jesus Christ. We are not called to isolate ourselves from the world, but we can insulate ourselves in it!

PARTNER WITH US!

"The Global Church is moving from parenting to partnering like never before. Our Lord has raised up this ministry to help us to synergize, mobilize, in order to finalize the Great Commission. Yet we realize that no organization can accomplish this alone. Every monthly partnership empowers us to plant churches and develop leaders in every nation. I invite you to join us in the global effort."

James O. Davis
Founder / Cutting Edge International
Founder / Global Church Network

JamesODavis.com

PARTNER WITH US!

Every $100 helps Global Church Network to **adopt an unreached people group**, who has **never heard the gospel for the first time!**

PLEASE CONSIDER MONTHLY SUPPORT
TODAY!

GCNW.tv/giving

The Global Church Network is the premier community pastors and Christian leaders from 2,700 denominations and 700,000 plus local churches. GCN brings the finest teaching though the Global Church Divinity School (GCDS.tv) and faith-filled training through its Global Hubs of Christianity. GCN synergizes Christian leaders and mobilizes the Body of Christ to finalize the Great Commission!

GCNW.tv

GLOBAL CHURCH DIVINITY SCHOOL®
PART OF THE GLOBAL CHURCH NETWORK®

IN THE FUTURE, WHO YOU STUDIED WITH IS MORE IMPORTANT THAN WHERE YOU STUDIED.

THE BEST **GLOBAL CHURCH CLASSROOM** IN THE WORLD!
190 World Class Faculty

GCDS.TV

GLOBAL CHURCH DIVINITY SCHOOL

PART OF THE GLOBAL CHURCH NETWORK

250+ Interactive Training Courses

5 Membership Levels

ONLY
$82 per month

Sign Up Today!

GCDS.TV

NOTES

NOTES

NOTES

NOTES

NOTES

NOTES